JUST ENOUGH SECURITY:

INFORMATION SECURITY FOR BUSINESS MANAGERS

JUST ENOUGH SECURITY:

INFORMATION SECURITY FOR BUSINESS MANAGERS

BY
TOM OLZAK, MBA, CISSP, MCSE

Copyright © 2006 by Thomas W. Olzak. All rights reserved. Except as permitted under the United States Copyright Act of 1976, no part of this publication may be reproduced or distributed in any form or by any means, or stored in a database retrieval system, without the prior written permission of the publisher.

Published by Erudio Security, LLC

Phone: 888-521-3780 Ext. 101
Fax: 888-521-3780
Email: inquiries@erudiosecurity.com

Web: www.adventuresinsecurity.com and www.erudiosecurity.com

To my wife, Ok Hui, whose love and support have made my life and this book possible...

TABLE OF CONTENTS

ACKNOWLEDGMENTS xiii
INTRODUCTION xv
PART I PRIMERS 1
CHAPTER 1 NETWORK PRIMER 3
   THE BASICS 4
      How data is formatted *4*
      Ethernet packets and MAC addressing *7*
      TCP/IP *8*
   NETWORKS 11
      Peer-to-peer *12*
      Hub centric networks *12*
      Switched networks *17*
      Routed networks *20*
   WIDE AREA NETWORKS AND THE INTERNET 23
   WIRELESS CONNECTIVITY 31
   CHAPTER SUMMARY 33

CHAPTER 2 INFORMATION SECURITY PRIMER 35
   THE EVOLUTION OF TECHNOLOGY AND THE RISE OF INFORMATION SECURITY 36
   INFORMATION SECURITY 41
      Confidentiality *42*
      Integrity *44*
      Availability *45*
      Risk management *47*
   ELEMENTS OF A SECURITY PROGRAM 47
      Prevent *49*
      Detect *51*
      Recover *54*
   CHAPTER SUMMARY 57

CHAPTER 3 RISK MANAGEMENT PRIMER 59
   RISK 60

RISK MANAGEMENT 61
   Reject.. *63*
   Accept... *63*
   Transfer.. *63*
   Mitigate.. *63*
THE RISK ASSESSMENT PROCESS.. 65
   The process.. *66*
   Define the system.. *67*
   Identify potential threats *71*
   Identify system vulnerabilities.. *73*
   Determine probability of occurrence, business impact, and risk................... *74*
   Evaluate... *82*
   Manage.. *84*
   Measure... *86*
CHAPTER SUMMARY 89

PART 2 JES.. 91

CHAPTER 4 THE JES SECURITY MODEL 93

JUST ENOUGH SECURITY 94
JUST ENOUGH SECURITY 94
   Management support.. *95*
   Security program... *95*
   User awareness *96*
   Physical access controls... *97*
   Firewalls *98*
   IPS/IDS... *98*
   Logical access controls *99*
   Antivirus software *101*
   Patch management *102*
   Device configuration *103*
PUTTING IT ALL TOGETHER 104
CHAPTER SUMMARY 105

CHAPTER 5 MANAGEMENT SUPPORT, DEVELOPING A SECURITY PROGRAM, AND USER AWARENESS.. 107

MANAGEMENT SUPPORT... 108
SECURITY PROGRAM.. 110
   Types of security programs *110*
   Resource requirements *111*
   Building policies... *112*
   Policy implementation.. *115*
   Standards, guidelines, procedures, and baselines................................ *116*
USER AWARENESS 118
   Building an Awareness Program.. *119*
   Measuring results... *120*
CHAPTER SUMMARY 120

CHAPTER 6 ACCESS CONTROLS ... 123

WHAT ARE ACCESS CONTROLS? ... 124
ADMINISTRATIVE CONTROLS ... 124
Preventive ... *125*
- Separation of duties ... 125
- Business continuity and disaster recovery planning/testing ... 125
- Proper hiring practices ... 125
- Proper processing of terminations ... 126

Detective ... *128*
- Security reviews and audits ... 128
- Mandatory vacations ... 129
- Background investigations of existing employees ... 130
- Rotation of duties ... 130

PHYSICAL CONTROLS ... 131
Preventive ... *132*
- Alternate power sources ... 132
- Flood management ... 133
- Backups ... 133
- Fences ... 136
- Guards ... 137
- Locks ... 137
- Biometrics ... 139
- Location ... 144
- Fire suppression ... 144

Detective ... *147*
- Detectors ... 147
- Guards ... 147
- Fire detection ... 148

LOGICAL/TECHNICAL CONTROLS ... 148
Preventive ... *148*
- Access control software ... 148

Detection ... *151*

WIRELESS NETWORK ACCESS CONTROLS ... 152
REMOTE ACCESS ... 158
Firewalls ... *160*
- Static packet filtering ... 160
- Stateful packet inspection (dynamic packet filtering) ... 161
- Deep packet inspection ... 162

CHAPTER SUMMARY ... 164

CHAPTER 7 INTRUSION DEFENSE ... 165

THE NATURE OF THE THREAT ... 166
Deperimeterization ... *166*
CONFIGURATION AND PATCH MANAGEMENT ... 168
Risks Associated with Poor Configuration Management ... *168*
Building a Configuration Management Program ... *169*
- Assign a responsible team or individual ... 169
- Create secure standards and guidelines ... 170
- Create and maintain an on-going configuration management process ... 171

    Challenges to Effective Configuration Management 172
   INTRUSION DETECTION/PREVENTION 173
    NIDS 173
      Placement of sensors 173
      Signature detection 175
      Anomaly detection 176
      Active response 177
      So why use NIDS 177
    HIDS 177
    Problem with Intrusion Detection 178
   INTRUSION PREVENTION 178
    NIPS 178
    HIPS 181
      HIPS deployment 182
      HIPS vs. NIPS 183
      Benefits of a host-based approach 184
   IDS AND IPS AS A LAYERED DEFENSE 184
   MALWARE DEFENSE 186
    Types of Malware 186
      Spyware 187
    Malware Prevention and Removal 188
   PERSONAL FIREWALLS 190
   CHAPTER SUMMARY 191

PART 3 CONTINUITY MANAGEMENT 193

CHAPTER 8 BUSINESS CONTINUITY PLANNING 195

   WHAT IS BUSINESS CONTINUITY PLANNING 196
    The Five Phases to Business Continuity Assurance 196
      Phase I: Analyze 196
      Phase II: Assess Risks 198
      Phase III: Strategy and Plan Development 200
      Phase IV: Test the Plan 204
      Phase V: Manage Test Results 207
   CHAPTER SUMMARY 208

CHAPTER 9 INCIDENT MANAGEMENT 209

   THE PURPOSE OF INCIDENT MANAGEMENT 210
   THE PATH TO EFFECTIVE INCIDENT MANAGEMENT 210
    Preparation 211
      Develop an incident management policy 211
      Form one or more incident response teams 212
      Develop a communication plan 215
    Detect and Analyze 217
    Contain 219
      Forensics 221
    Eradicate 223
    Recover 223
    Control (Manage) 224

    Cause and effect diagram 225
    Action plan.. 228
CHAPTER SUMMARY 228

ACKNOWLEDGMENTS

I'd like to thank the following friends and associates for their help in reviewing this book and for their support during the course of the project:

Dave Olzak, MCSE, CCNA, JNCIA-IDP
Technical Manager (IP Communications)
Analysts International

Tony Olzak, CCIE, MCSE
Chief Technology Officer
CISP

David Hayes, CNE, Security+
Security Analyst

Dave Hopson, Security+
Security Analyst

Craig Hulbert
Senior Network Engineer

INTRODUCTION

If you're an experienced network engineer looking for detailed explanations on how to configure a router or firewall, this might not be the book for you. But if you're a business owner, business manager, or information systems manager interested in understanding how to develop, implement, and manage an effective security program, I encourage you to read on.

The key difference that separates this from other books is my experience working as and with business managers to identify and deploy the *right security* for an organization. By "right security" I mean the application of reasonable and appropriate safeguards that actually result in a return on your security investment (ROSI).

It seems that most of the literature on the application of security principles to protect information assets is directed at large enterprises with seemingly unlimited security budgets. So I decided to write this book to present an easy to understand security methodology that can be implemented without unreasonable implementation and management costs. I call this methodology the Just Enough Security (JES) Model.

The JES Model employs the concept of "security in depth," or "layered security," to protect information assets. This approach is based on the belief that no one safeguard can completely protect your assets from a highly motivated threat. It's a combination of safeguards working together that creates an environment *secure enough* to deter attempts to compromise the confidentiality, integrity, or availability of your information assets. To introduce the various layers in the model, this book is divided into three parts.

Part 1 of the book includes three primers for readers unfamiliar with fundamental concepts used throughout chapters 4 through 9. These primers include enough information to provide a basic understanding of the following:

- Computer networks (Chapter 1)
- Information Security (Chapter 2)
- Risk Management (Chapter 3)

Skip one or more of these chapters if you believe you already possess a command of the topics covered.

Upon completion of Parts 2 and 3, you will understand:

- The JES Model and its various components (Chapter 4)
- How to create and manage an effective security program (Chapter 5)
- The various devices and activities necessary to implement effective access controls, both physical and logical (Chapter 6)
- How configuration management works in concert with intrusion and prevention solutions to strengthen your security infrastructure (Chapter 7)
- The importance of Business Continuity and how to develop an effective Business Continuity Plan (Chapter 8)
- How to respond to incidents in a way that mitigates business impact and the probability of recurrence (Chapter 9)
- Overall, how to make smart decisions about how to spend your information security dollars

To assist in the implementation of concepts covered in this book, I provide various tools. These tools are downloadable from the web site, www.erudiosecurity.com. Microsoft Excel 2003 is required to use these tools.

In order to demonstrate how certain concepts in this book apply to an actual organization, I created a fictitious company. This company is an aggregate of many companies with which I've worked. It does not

Introduction

represent any specific business entity. Please review the following company description before proceeding to Chapter 1.

Erudio Sprockets, Inc. (ESI)

ESI manufactures gear wheels for various purposes. It is a small company, employing 250 people. Annual revenue is $120 million with an annual net profit of $1.2 million. ESI is privately held. Figure I-1 is ESI's management organization chart.

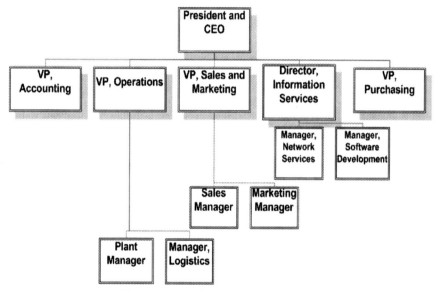

Figure I - 1: ESI Organization Chart

ESI has no dedicated security team. All security tasks are the responsibility of the Director of Information Services. The Manager of Network Services and the Manager of Software Development have been left pretty much on their own when it comes to providing security for information assets. Outside of Information Services, little attention is paid to safeguarding information or infrastructure.

Figure I-2 depicts ESI's information infrastructure.

Just Enough Security

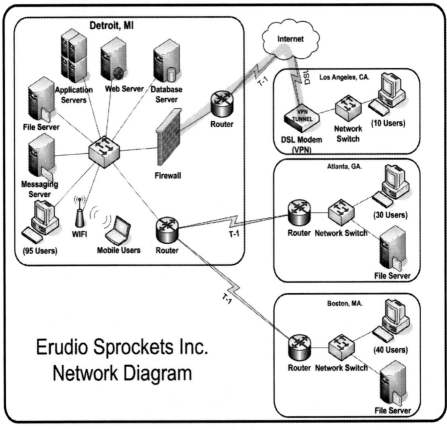

Figure I - 2

PART I
PRIMERS

CHAPTER 1
NETWORK PRIMER

It's not my intent to make you a network expert. The purpose of this chapter is to introduce basic concepts of networking. This mile-high understanding of how information flows around your organization is necessary before we discuss how to protect that information.

First, we'll look at how data is formatted. Next, we'll define a network at the most basic level. We'll then gradually expand the network with the introduction of additional network components and concepts. At the end of this chapter, you'll:

1. Understand how *data is formatted*
2. Understand *network fundamentals*
3. Understand how information is *transmitted* over a network
4. Understand how *hubs, switches, firewalls,* and *routers* are used and when each is the right answer for connecting network resources
5. Be able to discuss *LAN's, WAN's,* and the *Internet*
6. Understand how *wireless networks* work

It's not necessary to understand all the technical details in this chapter to understand the principles of Just Enough Security. Just focus on what you find interesting, and return to the following sections when you need additional information.

THE BASICS

In this section, we explore a few basic computing concepts we need to cover before launching into the world of networking. We also take a look at the format data takes as it travels between devices and how network addressing works. Throughout this book, we use the Ethernet standard to explain network principles.

> ### *Key Terms*
>
> ***Ethernet*** - *The most common local area network standard for exchanging data between networked devices. It defines how packets are sent and received. In Ethernet networks, devices are typically connected to the network via twisted pair copper wire, although fiber cable is often used.*
>
> ***Twisted Pair Cable*** – *Twisted Pair (TP) cable is made of pairs of copper wire. Each wire in a pair is twisted around the other wire in the pair to reduce electrical noise. The most common network TP cable is known as Cat 5 (Category 5). In an Ethernet network, Cat 5 cable is usually installed to support a speed of 100 Mbps (100 Megabits per second or 100 million bits per second). A variation of Cat 5, known as Cat 5e, can support faster speeds. TP cable is less expensive than fiber cable, but it is more sensitive to various types of electrical interference.*
>
> ***Fiber Cable*** *– Fiber cable is made of either plastic or glass. It's more expensive than copper network cable, but it's impervious to common types of electrical interference. Fiber cable also supports higher speeds and can be run across greater distances than copper.*

How data is formatted

All information in a computer is composed of **bits** (binary **digits**). A bit is a 1 or a 0, which is represented in a computer's circuits as the presence (1) or lack (0) of voltage. A collection of eight bits, known as a **byte**, represents a value in Base 2 (see *Base 2 Number System*). In order for one device on a network to properly interpret the bytes sent from another device, they must share a common coding format that defines the meaning of each byte value. The most common of these formats is **ASCII** (American Standard Code for Information Interchange). Windows-based systems typically use this format. Table 1 is a partial list of ASCII codes and the symbols, letters, and numbers they represent.

Network Primer

Code (Byte)	Code (Decimal)	Character	Code (Byte)	Code (Decimal)	Character
00100000	32	(SPACE)	01001000	72	H
00100100	36	$	01001001	73	I
00100101	37	%	01001010	74	J
00110000	48	0	01001011	75	K
00110001	49	1	01001100	76	L
00110010	50	2	01001101	77	M
00110011	51	3	01001110	78	N
00110100	52	4	01001111	79	O
00110101	53	5	01010000	80	P
00110110	54	6	01010001	81	Q
00110111	55	7	01010010	82	R
00111000	56	8	01010011	83	S
00111001	57	9	01010100	84	T
01000001	65	A	01010101	85	U
01000010	66	B	01010110	86	V
01000011	67	C	01010110	87	W
01000100	68	D	01011000	88	X
01000101	69	E	01011001	89	Y
01000110	70	F	01011010	90	Z
01000110	71	G			

Table 1 - 1: Partial ASCII Table

To a computer, the word HELLO would look like the collection of bits shown in Figure 1-1.

H	E	L	L	O
01001000	01000101	01001100	01001100	01001111

Figure 1 - 1: HELLO in Binary ASCII Values

Base 2 Number System

When we were very young, we began to learn how to manipulate the Base 10 number system. In Base 10, we use digits from 0 to 9 to represent quantities. Note that the highest digit is one less than the base value. The position of the digit in a number determines how many 10s or units it represents. For example, the number 1 represents one unit. If, however, we move the 1 one position to the left as in 10, it now represents 1 ten with 0 in the units position. The number 20 represents 2 tens and 0 units. The number 100 represents 10 tens. Another way to show the value of each position is the following:

$$...10^4 \mid 10^3 \mid 10^2 \mid 10^1 \mid 10^0$$
(Any number raised to the power of 0 equals 1)

Each position represents a power of ten. The number 234 can be broken down as:

$$(2 \times 10^2) + (3 \times 10^1) + (4 \times 10^0) = 200 + 30 + 4 = 234$$

Using a different base number system is as easy as replacing the 10's in our example above with the base number. In Base 2, or binary, powers of the number 2 are used to represent quantity. Unlike Base 10, Base 2 has only two digits, 0 and 1. Let's write 234 in Base 2.

First, we construct a table showing positional values based on powers of 2.

$2^7 =$	$2^6 =$	$2^5 =$	$2^4 =$	$2^3 =$	$2^2 =$	$2^1 =$	$2^0 =$
128	64	32	16	8	4	2	1

Next, we enter a combination of 1's and 0's so that the sum of the values equals 234.

$2^7 =$	$2^6 =$	$2^5 =$	$2^4 =$	$2^3 =$	$2^2 =$	$2^1 =$	$2^0 =$
128	64	32	16	8	4	2	1
1	1	1	0	1	0	1	0

So,
$11101010 = (1 \times 128) + (1 \times 64) + (1 \times 32) + (0 \times 16) + (1 \times 8) + (0 \times 4) + (1 \times 2) + (0 \times 1) = 234$

Ethernet packets and MAC addressing

Within a single computing device, ASCII-coded bytes work fine. But when those bytes of data have to move to other devices, we have to wrap some management information around them. This is the function of a network packet. Devices in an Ethernet network use Ethernet formatted packets to exchange data. A sample Ethernet packet is shown in Figure 1-2.

Destination Address	Source Address	Control/ Management Information	Data	CRC

Figure 1 - 2: Ethernet Packet Format

Each packet is divided into multiple segments. The first segment contains 6 bytes that make up the MAC address of the device to which the packet is being sent. The Source Address segment is comprised of 6 bytes that make up the MAC address of the device sending the packet.

A MAC (Media Access Control) address is a unique identifier written into every NIC (Network Interface Card) by its manufacturer. A NIC is installed in every network device. It's used to connect a device to the network. Devices on the same network segment use their MAC addresses to communicate with each other. A MAC address is required in addition to an IP address. While an IP address (covered later in this chapter) is required to get a packet to the proper segment, the packet can't make the final trip to the target device unless the packet contains the target device's MAC address.

A MAC address, also known as a hardware address, is composed of 16 bytes. The first 3 bytes are assigned by the IEEE (Institute of Electrical and Electronics Engineers, Inc.) to the manufacturer of the NIC; it uniquely identifies the manufacturer. The last 3 bytes are assigned by the manufacturer to uniquely identify each NIC it produces. Each NIC on a network segment must have a unique MAC address. Duplicate addresses, while rare, are normally caused by manufacturing errors. The following is a sample MAC address expressed in Base 16 (hexadecimal), format:

00-0D-60-3B-4F-88

The Control/Management segment contains 5 bytes that contain the length of the packet, transmission control information, and other low-level packet management information that helps the receiving device properly process the packet and return a response to the sending device.

The Data segment contains the actual application or file data. It also contains the information necessary to move a packet between network segments. The number of bytes in this segment is variable. It's determined by network management personnel during setup and optimization of the network. The **CRC** is a 4-byte value used to ensure that the packet is received by the target device without errors.

How a CRC works

A CRC (Cyclic Redundancy Check) is a value calculated by both the sending and the receiving device. The sending device runs the packet segments through a program that produces a value. This value, the CRC, is appended to the end of the packet before the packet is sent. When the receiving device picks up the packet, it also runs the packet (without the CRC) through the same program to produce its own CRC value. The receiving device compares the CRC it calculated to the CRC the sending device appended to the packet. If they don't match, the receiving device knows that the packet retrieved from the network was somehow changed or damaged in transit.

TCP/IP

A MAC address is fine for moving data around the same network segment. But it doesn't work very well when you want to send data to another segment. When traversing multiple network segments is necessary, using the TCP/IP suite of protocols is the most common way to get it done.

Key Terms

Bandwidth *– The capacity of a network or network segment. It may be described as bits per second or packets per second. The bandwidth of a network determines how much data passes a given point during a given period.*

Network Segment *– A portion of the network where all the devices share bandwidth. A network segment is sometimes known as a collision domain. A large network is usually separated into multiple segments to minimize collisions.*

Collision *– When two devices in the same Ethernet network segment attempt to*

Network Primer

send a packet at the same time, a collision occurs. Each device waits a random period before attempting to transmit again.

Collision Domain *– A network segment in which the packets of two or more network devices may collide when transmitted at the same time.*

Protocol *– A set of standards that defines how data should be formatted and processed in order for network devices to communicate with each other.*

TCP/IP (Transmission Control Protocol/Internet Protocol) is used by the Internet and by most businesses to move information between network segments. One major advantage of using a common set of protocols to move information over the Internet is a seamless integration with vendor and customer networks connected via a common global network. A major disadvantage is the ease with which crackers can use this global connectivity to spread malicious programs. We'll cover this in later chapters.

TCP/IP uses an IP addressing scheme to route packets from one network segment to another; it's known as a routable protocol. Figure 1-3 shows where the TCP/IP information is located in an Ethernet Packet. As you can see, the Data segment of an Ethernet packet in a TCP/IP network is actually an IP Datagram.

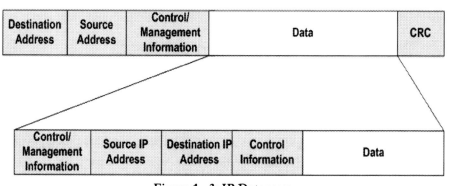

Figure 1 - 3: IP Datagram

Some of the items contained in the Control/Management section of the Datagram include:

1. The version of TCP/IP used to construct the Datagram
2. The length of the Control/Management section of the Datagram

3. The length of the Datagram
4. Time to Live (This is defined as the number of routers a packet can pass through before it's expired, also measured as "hops.")

The Source IP Address section contains the IP address of the sending device. The IP address of the target device is contained in the Device IP Address section. The second Control section may contain additional information about how to process the Datagram, or it can be omitted. The Data section contains some additional management information as well as the actual application or file information being sent.

An IP address consists of four sets of eight bits called octets, but network engineers usually write the address in **dotted decimal notation**. Figure 1-4 shows both the binary and the dotted decimal formats for an IP address. Although a network device can easily divide and process the binary version of an IP address, we humans aren't quite so adept at manipulating Base 2 values. Luckily, we can use dotted decimal notation when entering and managing them.

10101101011111001110101100010110

173.124.245.150

Figure 1- 4: IP Address - Binary and Dotted Decimal Formats

One or more of the octets in an IP address represent the address of the network or network segment to which a device is connected. The remaining octets uniquely identify the device. In the example above, the first two octets specify the network on which the target device resides. The second two octets, or the host address, uniquely identify a device on that network. See Figure 1-5.

Network Primer

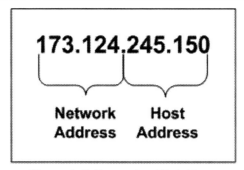

Figure 1- 5: Parts of an IP Address

So how does a network device know which octets represent the network portion of the address? This is accomplished through the use of a **subnet mask**. When configuring a network device with an IP address, you must also include a subnet mask. The mask tells the device how to split up the address. In our example, we used a mask of 255.255.0.0. Note that the mask is also presented in dotted decimal notation.

When the device applies the mask to the address, it treats each bit location where the mask contains a 1 as part of the network address. By applying the mask to the address, the device can determine the network address contained within the IP address. See Figure 1-6.

```
173.124.245.150 = 1 0 1 0 1 1 0 1 0 1 1 1 1 1 0 0 1 1 1 1 0 1 0 1 1 0 0 1 0 1 1 0
    255.255.0.0 = 1 1 1 1 1 1 1 1 1 1 1 1 1 1 1 1 0 0 0 0 0 0 0 0 0 0 0 0 0 0 0 0
Network Address = 1 0 1 0 1 1 0 1 0 1 1 1 1 1 0 0 or 173.124.0.0
```

Figure 1 - 6: Application of a Subnet Mask

We've covered the basic principles of data formatting and network addressing. It's time to apply this knowledge to learning how networks work.

NETWORKS

Before the introduction of networks, PC's were islands of information. To share information, a user copied information to a floppy disk and walked it to the person requesting it. This was affectionately known as a *sneaker net*. In addition, a printer was attached to each PC since there was no way for PC users to share computer devices. One of the biggest problems with this configuration was the lack of a central backup solution. Management had to rely on the diligence of each user to back up the information on his or her PC before leaving for the day. I doubt if anyone works in an office like this today. But it's nice to look back once in a while to see where we came from. Today's network technology has changed the way business information is stored, shared, and processed.

Peer-to-peer

Figure 1-7 shows a basic network configuration known as a peer-to-peer network.

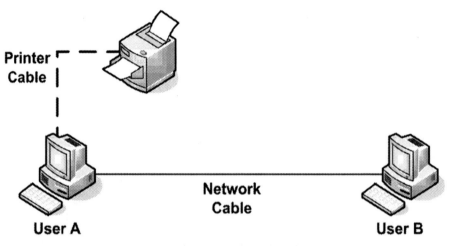

Figure 1 - 7: Peer-to-Peer Network

Each PC can use either its own internal disk storage, or it can share the storage of the other PC. Information is shared between the users of these two systems by each user granting file access to the other user. In addition, **User B** can use the printer connected to **User A's** PC. This configuration works well when there are few devices connected to your network. Peer-to-peer networks solve the problem of sneaker net and unshared resources in very small offices, but they quickly become unmanageable. Information might still be distributed across multiple systems, and a central backup process is typically not supported. I don't recommend this configuration for any size office. Figure 1-8 is a much better solution for connecting a small number of devices to a network.

Hub centric networks

Figure 1-8 depicts a network connected with a **hub**. This network configuration is a single network segment, a single collision domain, and a single broadcast domain. Network devices are normally connected to the hub with TP cable.

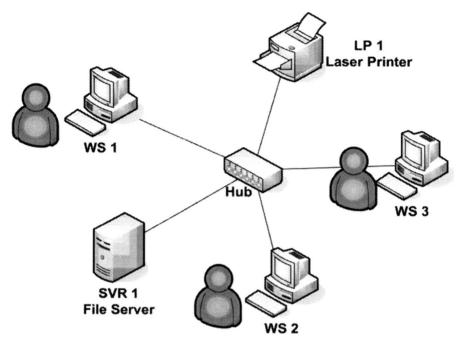

Figure 1 - 8: Hub-centric Network

All packets transmitted by the connected devices travel through the cables to the hub. Since all ports in a hub are effectively connected by a shared path (see Figure 1-9), all ports receive all transmitted packets. This results in each connected device seeing all packets, even those intended for other devices. Although a device won't process a packet addressed to another device, each NIC must examine the destination MAC address in each packet it sees to determine if the packet is intended for the device in which it's installed. The receipt of a large number of packets intended for other destinations can result in a very busy NIC. If a NIC is busy, performance suffers.

Just Enough Security

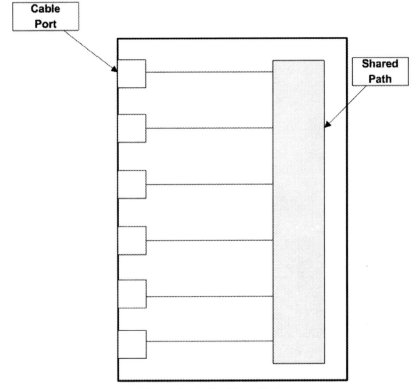

Figure 1 - 9: Inside a Hub

Another important difference between the network in Figure 1-7 and the network in Figure 1-9 is the presence of a **file server**. A file server is used to provide central storage of **flat file** information. Ensuring that critical information is backed up regularly is much easier. A file server can also double as a print server. All network PC's can use the server as a means to spool and print information to the shared **network-attached laser printer**.

Key Terms

Local Area Network – *A local area network (LAN) is a collection of devices connected together, over high speed links, to share computing resources. A LAN is typically deployed within a single office, building, or campus.*

File Server – *A file server normally stores flat files rather than large production databases. User home directories are normally located here. A file server can also*

> *provide network printing services. A server that performs both functions is called a file and print server. A print server allows multiple users on a network to share a printer.*
>
> **Flat File** – *In general, a flat file is a non-database file. We define a database as a production storage program such as Oracle or Microsoft SQL Server. Flat files include word processing documents, spreadsheet files, graphics, etc.*
>
> **Network-attached Laser Printer** – *A printer attached to a network via a network cable, with its own network address, is a network-attached printer. Using a print server, network users can share the printer.*

This is a good time to discuss how a device obtains the MAC address of a device on the same network segment with which it wants to communicate. Figure 1-10 is our hub-centric network with device IP addresses shown. The subnet mask for this network is 255.255.255.0. This means all the bits in the first three octets (counted from the left) are part of the network address. So the network address is 192.168.128.0. The fourth octet in each IP address is the unique device or host address.

In a Microsoft Windows environment, a list of network resources and their IP addresses is available to each connected device. WS 1 looks up SVR 1 in the list and retrieves the server's IP address.

Examining the IP address, WS 1 determines that the network address of SVR 1 is the same as its own network address. In other words, they are both in the same network segment. WS 1 checks the list of IP/MAC address pairs, called the Address Resolution Protocol (ARP) cache, it has incrementally constructed in its memory. The ARP cache contains addresses for all the devices with which WS 1 has recently communicated. In our example, SVR 1 is not contained in the list.

WS 1 sends a broadcast packet asking the device with IP address 192.168.128.1 to respond with its MAC address. Since this is a broadcast packet, all devices on the network, including the printer, process the packet. However, only SVR 1 responds with a MAC address.

When WS 1 receives SVR 1's MAC address, it stores it in its ARP cache for future use. It then creates an Ethernet packet with SVR 1's MAC address as the Destination Address and its own MAC address as the Source Address. WS 1 places the packet on the network.

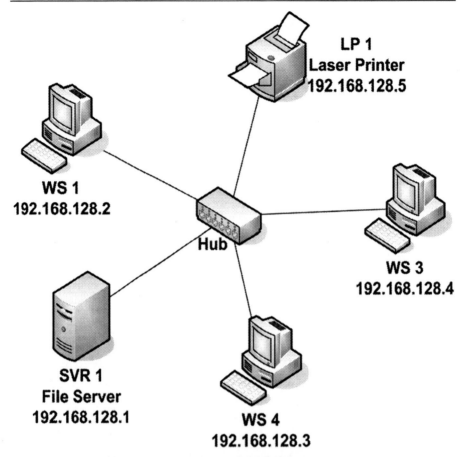

Figure 1 - 10: Hub-centric Network with IP Addresses

Every NIC in the network segment sees the packet and evaluates the Destination Address. Only SVR 1 will process the packet. If a response is required, SVR 1 uses WS 1's MAC address, included in the original packet, to return a packet.

If SVR 1 is in a different network segment with a different network address, additional steps are necessary. We cover these additional steps later in this chapter.

Since this is a collision domain, all connected devices are competing for the same bandwidth. In a small network, this is usually not an issue. In a large network, this can cause performance problems. One way to improve performance is to separate your network into multiple collision domains with a **switch**. Figure 1-11 depicts a common switched network configuration.

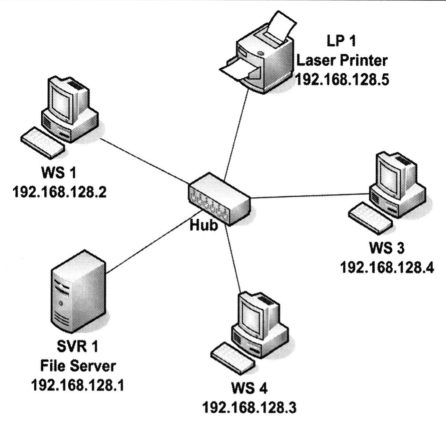

Figure 1 - 11: Switched Network

Switched networks

A network switch differs from a hub in one very important way; it stores in memory the MAC addresses of the devices connected to it and the port to which each MAC address is attached. This enables it to limit the sending of packets to only the port on which the target devices are located. The other ports are ignored.

Each port on the switch creates a separate collision domain; a packet is presented to only the devices connected to the same switch port. Broadcasts are an exception. Broadcast packets are sent out of every switch port. Therefore, our entire network in Figure 1-11 is still a single broadcast domain.

Just Enough Security

> ### Key Terms
>
> ***Email Server*** – *An email server is used to manage, send, and deliver email within your organization and across the Internet. To do this, it must run special email software, like Microsoft Exchange.*
>
> ***Database Server*** – *A database server is used to manage large amounts of production data. Data in a database server are organized into tables and the tables into databases. The software used to manage the databases is commonly called a Database Management System, or DBMS. Microsoft SQL Server is an example of a DBMS.*

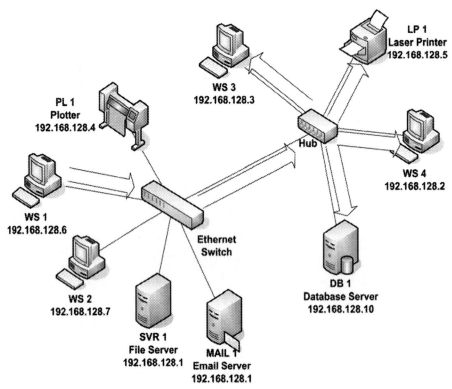

Figure 1 - 12: Addressed Packet Delivery in a Switched Network

Figure 1-12 shows an example of a packet sent from WS 1 and addressed to DB 1. The packet travels from WS 1 to the switch. Notice that WS 2, SVR 1, PL 1, and MAIL 1 didn't see the packet, because each of them is attached to its own switch port; each of them is on its own collision domain.

The switch examines the packet, determines the port to which DB 1 is attached by looking up DB 1's MAC address in its memory, and forwards it. In this case, the packet travels to the hub. The hub has no MAC address. Instead, the switch sees the MAC addresses of the devices connected to the hub. Since packets moving through a hub are delivered to all ports, all devices connected to the hub receive the packet. Figure 1-13 shows the path taken by a return packet.

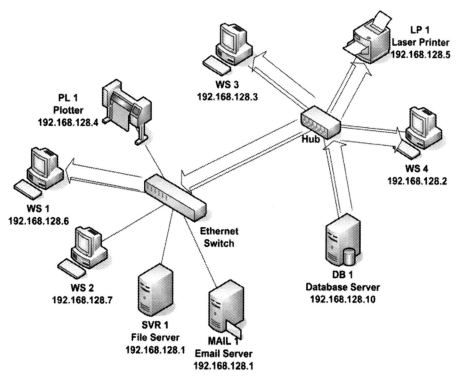

Figure 1 - 13: Switched Network Return Packet

A return packet from DB 1 to WS 1 travels back to the hub where it's distributed to all devices in the collision domain, including the switch. Once the packet reaches the switch, it's examined, the MAC address located, and then sent out the appropriate port to WS 1. Once again, WS 2, SVR 1, PL 1, and MAIL 1 are not bothered by unwanted traffic. By dividing your network into multiple collision domains through the use of a switch, you minimize the amount of unnecessary traffic each NIC must

Just Enough Security

examine. You also reduce the number of collisions and retransmits. As we'll see later in this book, segmenting your network with a switch can also help prevent packet captures by uninvited guests.

Routed networks

Another way to segment a network is with a **router**. The primary purpose of a router is to connect two or more network segments, while routing incoming packets to the appropriate segment. In addition to routing, routers differ from switches by not allowing broadcasts to pass from one segment to another. This feature further reduces unwanted traffic passing by each NIC.

Key Terms

Hop *– In a routed network, a hop is typically a router in which the datagram is inspected and sent on to the next step in its journey to the target device.*

Subnet *– A portion of a network in which all devices share a common network address.*

Application Server *– Users can attach to an application server to run a business program. The program actually runs on the server while sending the results to the users' workstations. In many cases, an application server is connected to a database server where the data processed is actually stored.*

Routing is the movement of IP Datagrams from one network segment to another. Routers make this happen by learning the network to which they're attached so that they route each datagram to the appropriate next **hop**. Let's take a look at an example depicted in Figure 1-14.

There are four routers: R1, R2, R3, and R4. There are also three servers and two workstations. The entire network uses a subnet mask of 255.255.255.0. So the first three octets of each IP address is the network segment address. The routers separate the network into nine network segments, or **subnets**:

> 192.168.125.0   192.168.250.0   172.16.5.0
> 192.168.128.0   172.16.2.0
> 192.168.130.0   172.16.3.0
> 192.168.140.0   176.16.4.0

Network Primer

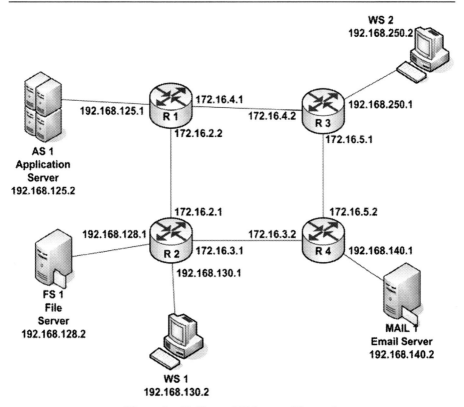

Figure 1 - 14: Routed Ethernet Network

Note that the connections between routers are actually subnets with their own network addresses. Each router interface is assigned an IP address.

If WS 1 wants to send a packet to MAIL 1, it creates an IP Datagram with a Destination IP Address of 192.168.140.2 and a Source IP Address of 192.168.130.2. Using the subnet mask, WS 1 calculates that the destination subnet is 192.168.140.0. Comparing this address to its own subnet address of 192.168.130.0, WS 1 knows that MAIL 1 is on a different subnet. WS 1 also knows that to get to a device on another subnet, it must use its **default gateway**. A default gateway is the address of a router port on a workstation's own subnet, which the network engineer configures when setting up the workstation's TCP/IP configuration. If a workstation is not configured with a default gateway, it can only communicate with devices on its own subnet. In this case, WS 1 is configured with the default gateway address of 192.168.130.1.

As we've seen in previous examples, one network device can't communicate with another network device unless it knows its MAC address. WS 1 looks in its ARP cache to see if it has the MAC address associated with 192.168.130.1. Since it hasn't recently communicated with that IP address, it doesn't have the proper MAC address. So WS 1 sends a broadcast packet onto its subnet asking the device with IP address 192.168.130.1 to return its MAC address. R2 responds with the MAC address of its port with that IP address. WS 1 constructs an Ethernet packet with the MAC address of its default gateway as the Destination Address and its own MAC address as the source address. It then sends the packet to R2.

When R2 receives the packet, it extracts the IP Datagram and applies the subnet mask to the Destination IP Address. Since routers in a network communicate information to other routers on the network about attached subnets, R2 knows that to get to subnet 192.168.140.0 it should route the packet to R4 address 172.16.3.2. R2 looks in its memory to see if it has the MAC address associated with that IP address. Since it has recently communicated with that port, it has the proper MAC address. If the MAC address hadn't been in memory, R2 would have placed a broadcast MAC address request on subnet 172.16.3.0.

R2 reconstructs an Ethernet packet, containing the IP Datagram from WS 1, with the Destination MAC Address of port 172.16.3.2 on R4 and a Source MAC Address for the R2 port with an IP address of 172.16.3.1. R2 places the packet on subnet 173.16.3.0. When R4 receives the packet, it extracts the IP Datagram. Once again, the subnet mask is applied to the Destination IP Address. This time, R4 knows that subnet 192.168.140.0 is connected to one of its ports.

Checking its ARP cache, R4 locates the MAC address for 192.168.140.2. It reconstructs an Ethernet packet with a Destination MAC Address for MAIL 1 and a Source MAC Address containing the MAC address of router port 192.168.140.1. R4 places the packet on subnet 192.168.140.0. MAIL 1 receives the packet, and extracts the IP Datagram and the transmitted data. Remember that the Destination IP Address and the Source IP Address have not changed as the IP Datagram was routed across the network. Because of this, MAIL 1 knows where to send a return packet.

There is one more important thing to know about routed networks. If designed properly, information can be routed around failing subnets. For example, if subnet 172.16.3.0 had been unavailable, the IP Datagram from WS 1 would have been routed to subnet 172.16.2.0, to subnet

172.16.4.0, and finally to subnet 172.16.5.0.   Typically, data is routed across the shortest path available.

WIDE AREA NETWORKS AND THE INTERNET

Many organizations have two or more locations that are too far apart to connect with high speed LAN connections. In these situations, a Wide Area Network (WAN) is used. Figure 1-15 shows a common configuration used to connect two locations.

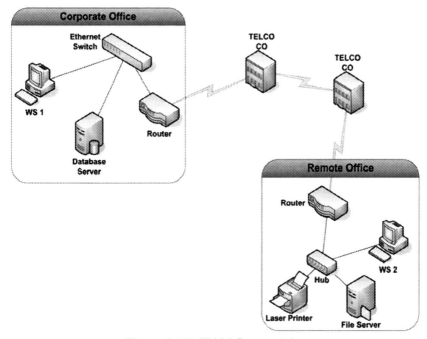

Figure 1 - 15: WAN Connectivity

In our example, two Ethernet LANs are connected with a T1. A T1, also known as DS-1, is a very common data circuit. It supports bandwidth of up to 1.544 Mbps. Compare this to the common 100 Mbps bandwidth for LANs. The T1 depicted in Figure 1-15 is a point-to-point circuit. One end of the T1 is connected to a **Telco CO**. The other end is connected to a **Smart Jack** in the remote office. A smart jack is the point at which the Telco terminates the T1 in your building. It's also the point at which the Telco's responsibility for support ends. This is known as the **Demarc**, short for Demarcation Point. Routers are used to connect the two LANs. Although some additional configuration and provisioning may be necessary, the manner in which these routers move packets between the two locations is essentially the same as that used by routers on a LAN.

> ### Key Terms
>
> ***Telco*** *– Telephone Company. Telco typically refers to local carriers rather than long distance carriers, although the separation between these two types of voice service providers is rapidly disappearing.*
>
> ***CO*** *– Central Office. A CO, sometimes called a switching station, serves two functions. First, it is the place where local circuits, both data and voice, are terminated into the Telco's network. Second, voice and data are transmitted from one CO to another until arriving at their destination. A CO may also serve as the point where voice and data traffic are transferred, or handed off, to another Telco's network.*

If an organization has a large number of remote locations, point-to-point connections may be far too costly. Other technologies are available to reduce costs in these situations. We'll discuss two of them—frame relay and IP VPN. Figure 1-16 depicts a frame relay solution.

Network Primer

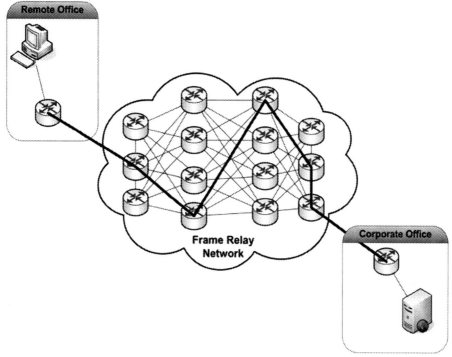

Figure 1 - 16: Frame Relay Connected Offices

A **frame relay** network allows multiple businesses to share a network of routers and switches to move data between locations. This can result in lower WAN costs when compared to point-to-point T1 connections. To connect two offices, like the one in our example, four components are necessary—a T1 connected to the Corporate Office, a T1 connected to the remote office, a Telco frame relay network, and a Permanent Virtual Circuit (PVC). We've already discussed how T1's are connected to a business office location.

Frame relay networks are very common today. Any Telco you call will have a solution similar to its competitor. The primary differences will be cost, support, and the effort required to roll the solution out to your facilities.

A **PVC** is a Private Virtual Circuit that connects two of your locations. To your network, it looks like a point-to-point connection. Other businesses sharing the frame relay network can't see your data. Your Telco provisions a PVC through router and switch configurations within their frame relay network. The bold path between routers in Figure 1-16 represents a PVC. The path provisioned may not be the most direct path. One of the objectives of provisioning is to minimize congestion in the network.

Although frame relay networks have been the solution of choice for many years, **IP VPN** is becoming a popular replacement. IP VPN uses the Internet instead of a frame relay network to move data between locations. This results in much lower costs. Before we look at IP VPN, we should understand how the Internet works and how a single location connects to the Internet. Figure 1-17 is a logical representation of the Internet.

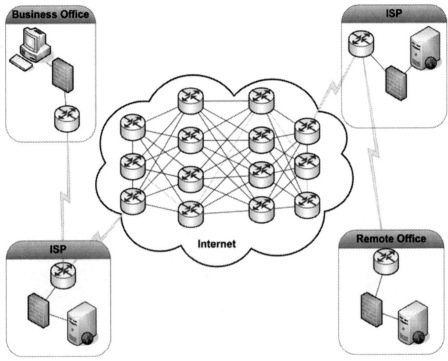

Figure 1 - 17: The Internet

The Internet is nothing more than a large web of interconnected routers and switches that move TCP/IP based packets from one of the millions of connected devices to another. Unlike a frame relay network, however, no PVC is provisioned. Each packet released to the Internet may travel a different path than the packet sent before or the packet sent after. There is also little you can do to mitigate the effects of congestion. But the improvements in Internet infrastructure have mitigated performance issues related to traffic patterns to the point where using the

Internet is often more cost effective than other forms of WAN connectivity.

Getting connected to the Internet isn't much different from how you connect your home; it's just on a larger scale with better service level expectations. Each of your facilities is connected to an Internet Service Provider (ISP). This may be the Telco you use to provide IP VPN services. The ISP is your portal to the Internet. (Although no CO is shown in our example, the circuits from the ISP's and the business locations still run through one or more CO's.) This is a straightforward setup. It's typically much cheaper than point-to-point or frame relay solutions; however, it does have one flaw. The Internet is not secure.

Traffic sent over the Internet can be picked up and read by anyone with access. In general, data is accessible at any hop between the source and destination locations. This isn't usually a problem if you're just browsing the Internet, but it can become a big problem if you are moving sensitive business information across the same infrastructure. This is where IP VPN comes in. Figure 1-18 represents an IP VPN implementation.

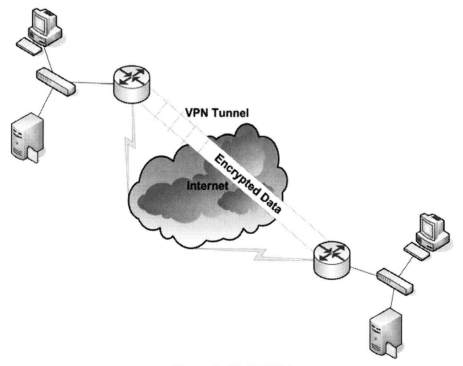

Figure 1 - 18: IP VPN

A router, firewall, workstation, server, etc. is configured at each location as a VPN endpoint device. Once configured, all packets transferred between these two devices are **encrypted**. The only part of the packet not encrypted is the information necessary to move it from one hop to the next. The encrypted data flow creates a virtual tunnel, shown in Figure 1-18 as the encrypted data pipe. You can use this connection as a private, secure WAN connection.

Not all connections to your business from the Internet are permanent, protected VPN connections; nor is the daily browsing by your employees probably anywhere close to secure. We'll detail using layered security to protect against Internet threats in later chapters. For now, we'll take a look at two common methods of isolating your critical network resources from the Internet. Figure 1-19 depicts a business location connected to the Internet via both a proxy server and a DMZ.

> ### Key Terms
>
> *Encryption* – *Encryption is the use of a key and a special algorithm to convert readable information into a form that is not readable unless you have the key to reverse the encryption process, or decrypt the information. The readable information is called* **clear text,** *and the encrypted information is called* **cipher text.**

A **proxy server** can serve many purposes. In this chapter, we'll take a look at four: packet filtering, network address translation (NAT), performance improvement, and site access control. We'll discuss packet filtering in more detail later in this chapter when we look at firewalls. We're using the proxy server in this example to block all traffic initiated by systems from outside our network. Only packets to devices within our network, that have initiated Internet connections, are allowed to pass.

NAT is a common service that allows an organization to present a small number of IP addresses to the Internet. These public facing addresses usually have nothing in common with the addresses of devices connected to the organization's LAN or WAN. When a device on the internal network initiates a connection to the Internet, the proxy server maps the device's private IP address to one of the publicly facing IP addresses. As far as a service on the Internet is concerned, it is communicating with the publicly facing IP address. It can't see the private IP address of the device with which it's communicating. This helps protect the organization's information assets since the outside

Network Primer

world doesn't know the IP addresses of the devices on the internal network.

Performance improvement is achieved through **caching**. When a user on your network accesses a web site, the proxy server can store a copy of the pages she views on its disk. If she or another user attempts to access that site again, the proxy server will check its cache to see if the requested page is stored there. If it is, the proxy server retrieves it and sends it to the requesting user. This is not only much faster than pulling it across the Internet but it also helps conserve circuit bandwidth.

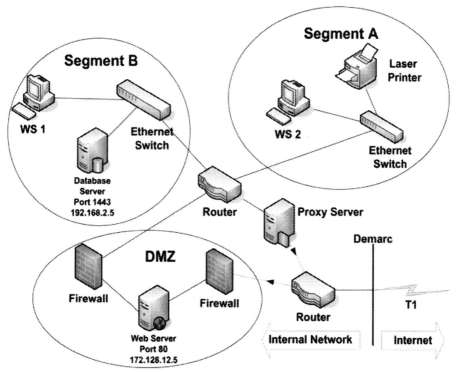

Figure 1 - 19: Internet Connectivity

Not all web pages can be cached. Pages that are dynamically built upon access, for example, can't be cached. Pages that can be cached should be refreshed periodically to ensure the content is up to date. Proxy servers can be configured to perform these updates automatically.

Finally, proxy servers can be used to restrict the sites to which an organization's users are allowed to connect. The capability of most proxy servers to perform this function is rather primitive. You can set up a proxy server to allow access to all web sites except those you enter into a list. The reverse is also true. You can set up the restrictions so your users can access nothing unless it's in the list. The management of these lists can become overwhelming. It's a better idea to implement one of the third party products that allow you to restrict Internet access by site category. Each category contains hundreds of sites the vendor has identified. The vendor provides daily updates to the category lists. Management is minimal.

The second way to connect to the Internet shown in Figure 1-19 is via a **DMZ**. The abbreviation DMZ is borrowed from the military term Demilitarized Zone. Like a military DMZ, a network DMZ serves as a guarded, fortified zone between the dangers lurking on the Internet and your internal network. These dangers include **crackers** and **malware**.

Key Terms

Cracker – *A cracker is someone who compromises the confidentiality, integrity, or availability of your network for personal profit.*

Malware – *Malicious Software. Malware includes trojans, viruses, and worms.*

In the example in Figure 1-19, the DMZ is used strictly to allow external access to certain databases. Many organizations require this kind of access for vendors or customers. Instead of providing direct access from the Internet to production databases, it's a better idea to provide access only to application/web servers in the DMZ. The servers in the DMZ are then granted restricted access to retrieve or write data to specified databases only. This functionality is provided by firewalls.

A **firewall's** primary role is to restrict traffic to only packets that meet certain criteria by using access control lists.

Access control lists are used by firewalls and routers to block all packets except those the business chooses to allow. The most common type of packet filtering uses source and destination IP Addresses and **ports** specified in the IP datagrams to determine whether to block a packet.

Ports

A port is an identifier that specifies the application or service that is supposed to receive a transmitted datagram. Some ports are assigned to specific applications.

Network Primer

For example, when a web browser communicates with a web server it uses port 80. Email uses port 25. Many ports are unassigned. They can be used by software developers or assigned dynamically by network devices when necessary to establish a session with another device.

In Figure 1-19, the external firewall is configured to allow only datagrams with a destination port of 80 and a Destination IP Address of 172.128.12.5 to pass into the DMZ. All other packets are blocked. Port 80 is used by the web application running on the web server in the DMZ. If a user coming in from the Internet opens the application and requests data, the web server will send a packet to the internal firewall with a Destination IP Address of 192.168.2.5 and port 1434. This is the address of the database server that hosts the application's data. 1434 is the port assigned to Microsoft SQL Server, a database management system on which the database is hosted. The internal firewall checks each packet it receives. In our example, it's configured with an access list that allows only traffic destined to 192.168.2.5, port 1434, and only if the source IP address matches that of the web server in the DMZ, 172.128.12.5. All other packets are blocked (dropped).

A DMZ is a very powerful tool to harden your network perimeter. In later chapters, we'll see that it's just one layer in a defense-in-depth strategy necessary to protect your information assets.

WIRELESS CONNECTIVITY

In recent years, mobile devices have become a large percentage of the end user devices used by workers to perform day-to-day tasks. These devices include Personal Digital Assistants (PDA's) and laptops. When a traveling user visits a satellite facility, or even the corporate office, it isn't very convenient to pull out a network cable, find a network connection under or behind someone's desk, and perform the gymnastics necessary to physically connect to the network. Users taking their laptops to conference rooms or into plant or warehouse environments often find there is insufficient network access. The cost of running network cable to every location where access is required can be rather high. Add to these issues the proliferation of technologies such as wireless voice over IP, radio frequency identification devices, wireless manufacturing devices, etc. and the significant improvements in productivity usually more than make up for the cost of a wireless LAN rollout.

Just Enough Security

Figure 1-20 shows an Ethernet network with **wireless access points**. An access point (AP) contains a radio receiver/transmitter to communicate with wireless end user devices. It's typically attached to a network via a network cable. In this example, the AP's are connected to a standard Ethernet switch with TP cable. An end user device must have a wireless NIC installed to connect to an AP. The NIC and the AP must support the same wireless protocols.

The average real-world range on a business class AP is between 150 and 200 feet. Quality of connectivity and maximum range are affected by environmental conditions. These conditions can include large metallic objects, electromagnetic interference (EMI) produced by machinery, or building materials.

Wireless connections create difficult security challenges. We'll discuss these challenges in later chapters.

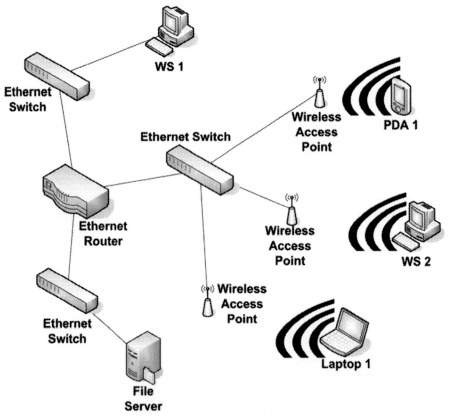

Figure 1 - 20: Wireless Connectivity

> ### *IEEE Wireless Protocol Standards*
>
> ***802.11b*** – *Supports up to 11 Mbps over the 2.4 GHz band.*
> ***802.11g*** – *Supports up to 54 Mbps over the 2.4 GHz band.*
> ***802.11a*** – *Supports up to 54 Mbps over the 5 GHz band.*
>
> *802.11b and 802.11g are commonly combined onto the same AP. The bandwidth supported decreases as the distance from the AP increases or as environmental conditions degrade. 802.11b has been around for some time and counts for a very large piece of the wireless networking world. Both 802.11b and 802.11g devices typically use the same access point. 802.11g devices connecting to an older 2.4 GHz AP that only supports 802.11b will connect at 11 Mbps.*
>
> *802.11a is not catching on very quickly. Its range, 60 to 100 feet, is much less than the 300 feet of 2.4 GHz technologies. This means that it will take more access points, and a bigger budget, to provide wireless connectivity in larger office environments. In addition, the 5 GHz radio is not compatible with 802.11b or 802.11g devices. So if you decide to install 802.11a AP's, you'll also have to replace all earlier technology wireless NIC's.*

CHAPTER SUMMARY

We walked through building a network from a peer-to-peer configuration to a routed network with WAN connectivity. We saw how the management of broadcast and collision domains can improve performance. You should also understand at an elementary level how information moves through a network.

At the beginning of this chapter, I stated that this is a basic view of networking. What I've tried to do is provide a basic understanding of how various components work together to create a network. It's through the proper implementation of these and other components—as well as policies, processes, physical security, and training—that you begin to protect your information assets.

If you find yourself wanting to learn more about networking, I recommend you pick up a book intended as a study guide for the CompTIA Network+ exam. I'm not necessarily suggesting you take the exam, but reading the material relevant to the exam will provide you with a solid understanding of network principles.

CHAPTER 2
INFORMATION SECURITY PRIMER

Upon completion of this chapter, you will be able to:

1. Discuss why information security has increased in importance during the past decade
2. Define *Information Security*
3. Describe the three areas of focus for a *Security Program*
4. Describe the three levels of prevention and detection security controls
5. Effectively apply controls using the principles of *Diversity in Design* and *Defense in Depth*
6. Discuss the principles of *Incident Management*

THE EVOLUTION OF TECHNOLOGY AND THE RISE OF INFORMATION SECURITY

In the early days of computing, securing information was relatively easy. Information was stored in a locked room, on a large **mainframe** computer, with a **proprietary operating system**, supporting tightly controlled remote access from known locations. Figure 2-1 depicts this type of environment.

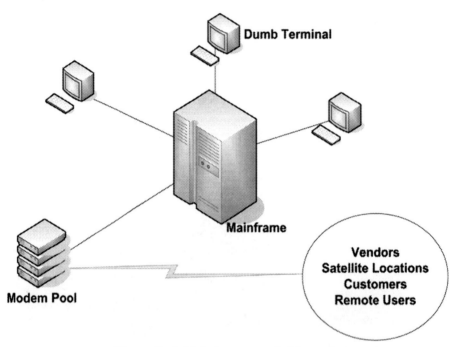

Figure 2 - 1: Mainframe-centric Network

The **dumb terminals** used to access applications and data on the mainframe were incapable of storing data locally; they had no disk drives. Viruses were unknown because information couldn't be loaded or downloaded to terminals, and the Internet wasn't a critical business network. Physical access to the mainframe was necessary to load programs. Even then, the permissions necessary to load applications were very tightly controlled. In addition, technology that allowed the easy download and removal of information, such as **thumb drives**, didn't exist. Access to the information on mainframes was effectively controlled by a few User IDs, passwords, and locked doors.

Key Terms

Mainframe – *A large, expensive, powerful computer. Early mainframe computers often filled an entire room. These systems became know as mainframes because the early models occupied a number of metal frames, the main one containing the processor and memory.*

Proprietary Operating System – *An operating system (OS) is an application that manages the processing activities of a computer. Microsoft Windows XP, Microsoft Windows Server 2003, and Linux are examples of operating systems. A proprietary operating system is written for a specific computer and cannot be run on any other system. For example, the IBM AS/400 ran an operating system called OS/400. OS/400, written and sold by IBM, could not be run on any other device but the AS/400. Compare this to a non-proprietary OS like Windows XP that can be run on many different platforms from a variety of vendors.*

Dumb Terminal – *A device consisting of a screen and keyboard, used for communicating with another computer, usually a mainframe. Unlike a personal computer, it has no local processing capabilities or disk storage.*

Thumb Drive – *A thumb drive is a small, compact, rewritable storage device that interfaces with a computer through high speed interfaces, such as a USB port.*

Modem Pool – *A modem pool is a group of modems that answer calls placed to a single phone number. Users can also use the modem pool to dial out to remote locations. Modem pools, or other types of dial-up devices, were popular for remote terminal and personal computer access to centralized business systems prior to the introduction of Internet-based technologies.*

The next major innovation in business processing was the personal computer (PC). The PC introduced new security concerns. First, much of an organization's processing was moved to the PC. Unlike dumb terminals, PC's had local processing capabilities and local storage devices. In addition, PC's provided opportunities for placing confidential information on removable storage, such as a floppy disk, which could be easily moved to unauthorized locations.

Second, organizations began to connect PC's together in LANs. This allowed the movement of information between PC's and a mainframe. See Figure 2-2. As more and more information moved about an

Just Enough Security

organization, there were additional opportunities for it to be intercepted by unauthorized individuals.

Third, PC's introduced non-proprietary OS's, like MS-DOS. (Microsoft Disk Operating System). With the proliferation of these OS's came the birth of viruses. Early viruses were spread by floppy disk sharing or by moving files from one PC to another over the LAN.

Finally, PC's were frequently equipped with modems. Connecting a simple telephone line to one of these communication devices provided users with access to the outside world. Although the Internet didn't exist, threats to information security were still downloaded into business environments by unsuspecting business users.

Like with the mainframe-only environment, security was primarily provided by User IDs, passwords, and locked doors. The mainframe remained the primary center for the processing and storage of critical business information.

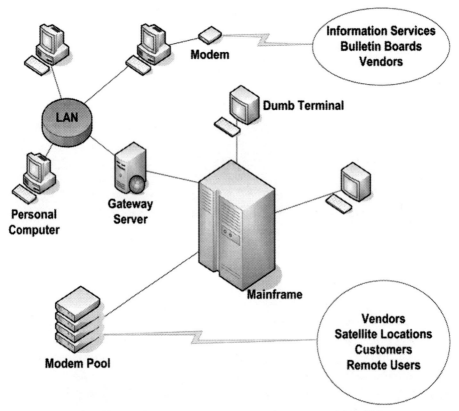

Figure 2 - 2: Mainframe-centric Environment with LAN

Information Security Primer

> ### Key Terms
>
> **Gateway Server** – *At the most fundamental level, mainframes and PC's use different coding standards to process information and different protocols for communication. The gateway server acts like an interpreter, helping the PC's and the mainframe understand each other.*

Over time, the simple PC evolved into a PC server. The combination of the processing power of the PC server and the convenience and flexibility of desktop PC's led to less dependence on the more costly and proprietary mainframe. Dumb terminals were gradually replaced by PC's. Figure 2-3 depicts a LAN centric network. The mainframe has become just another network attached device. The primary device used to access the mainframe has changed from the dumb terminal to the desktop PC. Modem pools were replaced by more flexible and secure remote access routers.

As LAN's grew, so did the decentralization of an organization's information. No longer was information stored in a centralized mainframe. Much of the information necessary to operate the business was located on multiple servers or desktop PC storage.

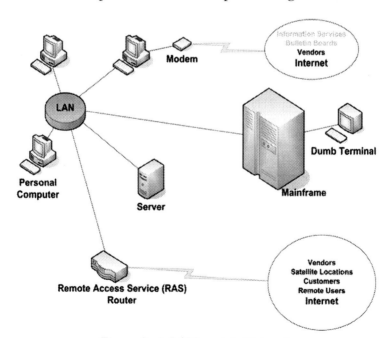

Figure 2 - 3: LAN-centric Network

One of the most significant developments, however, was the introduction of the Internet. This public, shared, global network was accessible from both controlled access points as well as uncontrolled access points, such as locally attached modems. Customers and vendors began insisting on business use of the Internet for email, file transfers, or simply providing general information about an organization. Along with vendors, customers, and employees, crackers also got busy transforming their viruses into worms and trojans that had the capability of moving effortlessly across the Internet's various nodes.

Today, the mainframe is usually absent from an organization's network. Instead, large businesses deploy hundreds of servers to process and store data. Figure 2-4 is a logical view of a modern network.

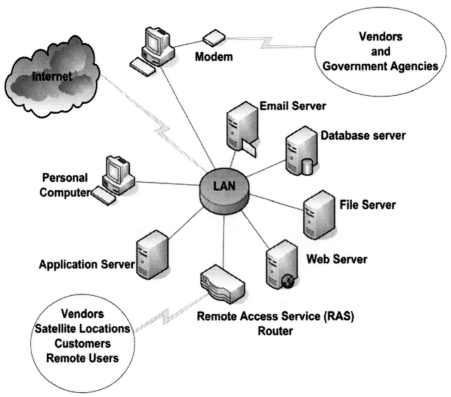

Figure 2 - 4: Modern Network

In today's networks, organizations must protect information as it travels across various network devices and is stored on a variety of storage media. In addition, there are multiple connections to the outside world that are less safe than in the past. For example, most organizations have a high-speed connection to the Internet. The Internet is like the Wild West; no one is in control and it's each person's responsibility to provide protection for himself. Many organizations have multiple locations, each with a LAN, storage, and outside connections. This significantly increases the risk to critical information.

Although the move from isolated, centralized processing to distributed, connected networks has improved business agility and productivity, it has also introduced a host of security challenges. This resulted in the elevation of Information Security from simple account management to an integral part of business operations.

INFORMATION SECURITY

Put simply, the proper application of information security ensures the confidentiality, integrity, and availability of information assets, in a reasonable and appropriate manner, through the proper application of risk management. Figure 2-5 depicts the relationship of the elements of information security.

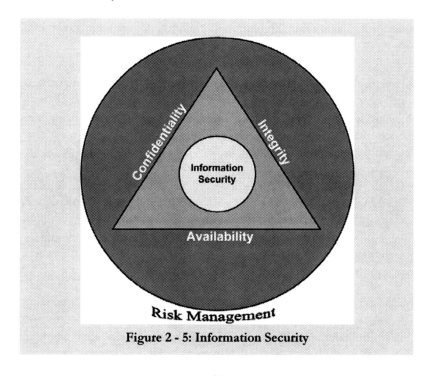

Figure 2 - 5: Information Security

Confidentiality

Confidentiality is the protection of information from unauthorized access by people, processes, or systems. Examples include access by employees who do not require the information to perform their daily tasks and access by non-employees for either malicious or non-malicious purposes.

An organization's information can usually be divided into that which the world can see and that which only employees can see. Employee viewed information should be further classified so that a "need-to-know" approach to accessing information is effectively applied. Security design in both processes and systems must include access controls with sufficient granularity to accommodate and restrict access to multiple information classification levels.

It isn't necessary to overly complicate information classification. I like to use three classification levels: critical, confidential, and public. Critical information includes documented intellectual property and information governed by regulations such as the Health Insurance Portability and Accountability Act of 1996 (HIPAA) and the Sarbanes-Oxley Act of 2002 (SOX). All other business information is included in the confidential category unless specifically marked as public.

There are many threats to confidentiality. The following list includes some of the most common ways information is compromised and ways to protect your business:

- **Unprotected Downloaded/Uploaded Files** – Information is stored in environments with controls commensurate with its classification level. This information may be moved or copied to another server or network. When this happens, the security controls of the new environment should be equal to or greater than the original environment.

- **Crackers** – A cracker is someone who bypasses an organization's security controls for the purpose of personal gain, revenge, or some other malicious intent. Strong layered prevention and detection controls must be in place to help defend against this type of attack.

- **Unauthorized User Activity** – Users with authorized access may intentionally or unintentionally browse sensitive information, which they don't need in order to perform their daily tasks.

Access controls tuned to information classification levels and employee roles help to protect against this type of threat.

- **Social Engineering** – Social engineering is one of the most serious threats to an organization. Managers can spend millions on sophisticated prevention and detection mechanisms only to have an unauthorized person obtain access to sensitive information through a simple telephone conversation or an email exchange. The social engineer uses deception to obtain sensitive information directly from an unsuspecting employee. A manager can do two things to help protect against this type of threat. First, ensure need-to-know is built into every access control. This limits the information any one employee can potentially compromise. Second, train your employees to properly handle requests for information. Security awareness training, covered later in this book, is your most effective defense against social engineering.

- **Trojan Horses** – A trojan horse is a type of **malware** that looks and acts like a normal application. A user might download it from the Internet as part of an application installation. However, a trojan will also perform some malicious activity. It might allow an unauthorized user to gain access to your network, or it might automatically copy files, over the Internet, to an attacker's storage device. The best defense against trojans is to restrict the installation of software to only authorized personnel. Management should implement this defense through the combination of policies, processes, and technology. Another critical defense is the use of anti-virus software. Under no circumstances should you have a system connected to your network that is not running an updated anti-virus program.

- **Spyware** – Spyware is a relatively new threat. It's normally downloaded, without user request, from Internet sites visited by your network users. Some spyware is installed without malicious intent. Other spyware may be installed to collect sensitive information and send it to an attacker's location. In any case, spyware will affect the performance of the system on which it's installed. The safest approach is to eradicate spyware wherever it's found on your network. You should also take steps to prevent its installation in the first place. Prevention steps include the implementation of anti-spyware appliances at the entry points to your network from the Internet, the use of **host intrusion prevention systems,** or the implementation of anti-virus products that incorporate the identification and eradication of spyware on individual systems.

- **Masquerading** – Masquerading is the use of an authorized user's ID and password by an unauthorized user to gain access to a network. Protecting passwords in addition to employee security awareness training focused on protecting network access information are a good start in thwarting this threat.

> ### *Key Terms*
>
> ***Host Intrusion Prevention System (HIPS)** – A HIPS is installed on a server, desktop, or laptop system. It may be configured to prevent certain actions from being performed or to report suspicious activities. Blocked actions include copying or moving files, deleting files, installing applications, etc. Any attempt to perform one of the restricted activities may result in a log entry or system administrator alert.*

Integrity

Protecting information integrity goes beyond preventing unauthorized viewing. Protecting the integrity of information requires the implementation of policies, processes, and technology that prevent or detect the unauthorized modification of data. Threats against integrity are the same as those that may compromise confidentiality. But there are additional steps managers can take to ensure data is not changed without proper authorization.

- **Enforce Least Privilege** – Users should have change access only where necessary to perform their day-to-day tasks.
- **Separation of Duties** – No single employee should be able to perform all tasks associated with a single transaction. For example, an employee in Payroll shouldn't be able to:
    - Create an employee account
    - Enter a manual payroll check

- o Approve the manual payroll check
- o Pick up the check for the named employee

Any one of the first three tasks moved to another employee will significantly reduce the risk of entering and processing unauthorized information. Separation of duties is based on the belief that the probability that two or more employees will collude to perform an unauthorized act is much less than a single employee performing the same act alone.

- **Rotation of Duties** – One of the best ways to prevent or detect unauthorized changes to data is to rotate employees through different roles. If an employee knows someone else will have access to the work she's done, she'll be less likely to perform an unauthorized or illegal act.

- **Application-only Data Access** – User access to data should be restricted to application interfaces. Direct database access should be allowed only for those directly responsible for database health, such as database administrators. Even then, managers should have controls in place to monitor database management activities.

Availability

Protecting the confidentiality and integrity of information is important. But your business can't operate unless your employees can access that information. The concept of availability addresses the ability of users to access information when and where they need it. There are two primary availability concerns when implementing information security in your organization: denial of service (DoS) and business continuity.

- **Denial of Service** -- DoS is typically caused by the actions of humans or software. In DoS, the attack agent uses all available processing resources. Authorized users are unable to access or process business information. Controls to prevent or detect DoS attacks include:

- Application of critical security patches
- Implementation of firewalls that drop all packets except those intended for verified and authorized connections with internal resources.
- Implementation of intrusion prevention/detection services

- **Business Continuity** – Business Continuity is concerned with natural and man-made events that may result in the loss of processing capabilities. Included are earthquakes, fire, floods, terrorist attacks, strikes, chemical spills, hardware or software failure, etc. Business continuity events can range from a failed hard drive to the destruction of the data center. Some of the actions you can take to mitigate the effects of these events include:
    - Development and testing of a Disaster Recovery Plan to restore services after a catastrophic event
    - Installation of fire detection and suppression systems that are designed to protect electronic equipment
    - Implementation of fault-tolerant hardware systems that allow the processing of data in the event of a hardware failure
    - Implementation and enforcement of a Change Management Process to ensure changes are made to production systems while mitigating the risk of causing system failure
    - Performing regular backups of data with off-site storage for backup media
    - Implementation of physical and logical controls to prevent unauthorized access that might lead to disruption of processing
    - Development and testing of an Incident Management Process, enabling rapid service recovery when a business continuity event occurs

Risk management

The application of the concepts of confidentiality, integrity, and availability should always be applied judiciously. This is the role of Risk Management. Risk management is the process of reducing and maintaining risk at an acceptable level through the use of a well-defined and actively employed security program. This security program should always weigh the business impact of a security incident against the cost of protecting against that incident. It's a wise manager who doesn't unnecessarily spend a large percentage of her working capital in an attempt to completely eradicate all system vulnerabilities. The concept of risk management is covered in detail in Chapter 3.

ELEMENTS OF A SECURITY PROGRAM

In order to effectively employ the information security concepts introduced in the last section, an organization must have a well documented and active security program. Chapter 5 is dedicated to learning how to build a security program. The purpose of this section is to provide a general overview.

A security program consists of **policies, procedures, standards**, and **guidelines** that define a framework upon which to build three basic types of security controls: prevention, detection, and recovery. Figure 2-6 shows the relationship between these layers.

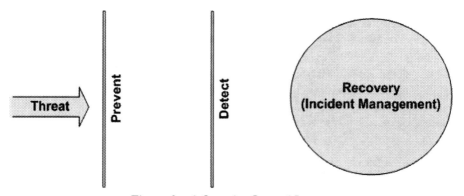

Figure 2 – 6: Security Control Layers

Just Enough Security

> ### *Key Terms*
>
> ***Policy*** *– A policy contains management's position on security issues. Developed to address issues at a high level, policies can include enterprise-wide security concerns or only issues pertaining to a specific system. Policies don't include detailed steps for building policy compliant systems. This is the role of procedures.*
>
> ***Procedure*** *– A procedure contains detailed, step-by-step instructions for building a secure system or system component. Procedures are written to consistently deploy systems that are compliant with management policies.*
>
> ***Standards*** *– These mandatory activities, rules, etc. support policies by specifying in detail how systems should be configured, deployed, and managed.*
>
> ***Guidelines*** *– Unlike standards, guidelines provide a discretionary framework. If a specific standard doesn't exist to cover a specific activity, guidelines can be used to determine the best course of action while maintaining policy compliance.*

The first layer of controls is designed to prevent a **threat agent** from exploiting a vulnerability resulting in business impact. Managing business impact and vulnerabilities are covered in Chapter 3. When presented with a threat, prevention controls attempt to block it from reaching its target. If the prevention controls fail to stop the threat agent, the second layer of controls is intended to detect the unusual activities that serve as warning signals that a security incident may be imminent or in process. If it's determined that a security incident is occurring, the third layer of controls is activated. These controls are designed to identify, contain, eradicate, and manage the threat agent and its effects, thus mitigating the impact on the business.

> ### *Key Terms*
>
> ***Threat Agent*** *– A threat agent is an entity or event that attempts to exploit one or more weaknesses in the security controls protecting an information asset resulting in an adverse impact on the asset's confidentiality, integrity, or availability.*

Within each of these control layers there are three control areas: physical, administrative, and technical. The following sections describe each of the control areas and the actual controls commonly deployed within them.

Prevent

Physical prevention controls are intended to prevent physical access by humans or to mitigate physical damage by natural or man-made events. Physical prevention controls include:

1. Backups
2. Fences
3. Man traps (see Figure 2-7)
4. Secure data centers and limited access to buildings through the use of badge systems, locks, etc.
5. Stationary or roving security guards
6. Alternative power sources, such as uninterruptible power supplies or generators
7. Proper selection of a site to minimize the effects of crime, political strife, natural disasters, etc.
8. Fire detection and suppressions systems – The proper selection of fire prevention and suppression systems is a big factor in the amount of damage caused by a facility fire. Chapter 6 describes various types of systems and guidelines for when to use each type.

Administrative controls implemented to prevent the success of threat agents focus on the management of people and processes. Common controls of this type include:

1. Policies, procedures, standards, and guidelines
2. Tested business continuity plans
3. Separation of duties

Administrative controls are explained in more detail in Chapters 3 and 4.

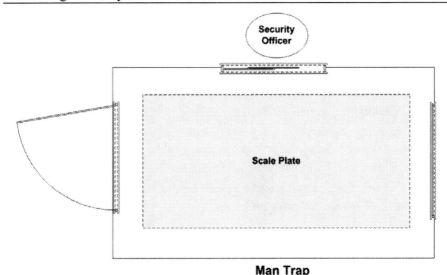

Man Trap
Figure 2 - 7

Key Terms

Man Trap – *A man trap is typically a small room with a door at each end that serves as an access point for a restricted facility. When a person enters one door, the other door is shut. A security officer is typically stationed at a window to check identification and to prevent* **piggybacking**. *If the security officer suspects that the person attempting to enter the facility is an intruder, she secures both doors, trapping the suspect until the police or other authorities respond. A scale can also be used to prevent piggybacking or the smuggling of contraband. If the weight on the scale appears to be too high, the security officer can take steps to investigate prior to opening either door.*

Piggybacking – *When an unauthorized person enters a restricted room or facility by passing through an open door or gate with an authorized person, this is called piggybacking. For example, an intruder may wait by a locked door until a person with a key card opens the door to enter the secure area. Prior to the door closing, the intruder simply passes through. Organizations with weak security awareness training programs may find that courteous employees actually hold the door for intruders.*

The third area of prevention controls consists of hardware and software. These technical controls, which are designed to block threat agents, include the following:

1. Smart cards – A smart card is a physical device about the size of a credit card that contains user authentication information. It's usually used in addition to a user ID and password. A user must have the smart card in his possession to log on to his PC or to the network.
2. Encryption – This is the conversion of readable plaintext information to unreadable ciphertext. Highly sensitive data should be encrypted both while traveling over the network and while at rest on a drive, tape, or other storage medium.
3. Operating system access controls
4. Passwords
5. Biometrics – This is the use of one or more biological attributes to identify a user attempting to authenticate to a system. These attributes include fingerprints, finger or hand geometry, retinal scans, and voice recognition.
6. Anti-virus and anti-spyware software
7. Intrusion prevention systems, both host and network based
8. Firewalls

These controls are covered in more detail in Chapter 6.

Detect

Controls in the same three areas are used to detect threat agents or their effects if the prevention controls fail. Physical detection controls include:

1. Motion detectors
2. Smoke and fire detectors
3. Security cameras
4. Sensors and alarms

Just Enough Security

As with administrative prevention controls, administrative controls designed to detect evidence of current or intended malicious activity against information assets are focused on management actions, including:

1. Rotation of duties
2. Security reviews and audits
3. Mandatory vacations (Mandatory vacations serve the same purpose as rotation of duties. Someone else must look at the work the vacationing employee has been doing.)
4. Performance evaluations
5. Background investigations

Finally, audit trails and intrusion detection systems are implemented to provide technical detection controls.

How prevention and detection controls are implemented is often just as important as the controls themselves. There are two primary principles that should govern your deployment of security controls: diversity in design and defense in depth.

The diversity in design principle deals with the degree of variety in your controls. By variety is meant not only the types of controls but also the number of vendors and approaches to various controls. Let's look at Figure 2-8 as an example.

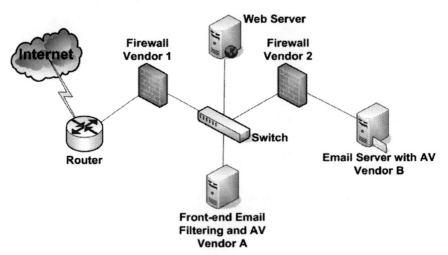

Figure 2 - 8: Diversity in Design

From the Internet, packets must travel through a firewall to reach the organization's DMZ. The DMZ is home for a web server and a front-end email server. Only packets destined for port 25 on the email filtering server or port 80 on the web server are allowed through the external firewall. However, it's possible for an attacker to crack the security of this device. If this happens, the attacker has access to all devices in the DMZ. Since the DMZ devices are **hardened** and contain no sensitive information, the attacker will most certainly attempt to get to the internal network where the pickings are usually easier and richer.

If both firewalls are the same model from the same vendor, the attacker's job is much easier. The actions she takes to crack the external firewall will probably work quite well in cracking the internal firewall. But in our example, the firewalls are from different vendors. This means that the techniques the attacker uses to crack the first firewall will probably not work on the second firewall. Since cracking a hardened firewall typically requires significant effort, the **work factor** associated with cracking two dissimilar firewalls may be too great for the attacker's liking. Diversity in design will increase the work factor to a level much higher than that of a network with a single vendor design.

There is often one big disadvantage to employing this approach to network defense. Your network team must understand multiple vendor device configurations. In this example, it might increase the total cost of ownership of the diverse firewalls.

Key Terms

Hardened *– A hardened device is one that is configured to run the minimal number of services or programs or that processes only packets that meet specific criteria. For example, steps for hardening a Windows server include disabling or deleting all unnecessary accounts, disabling all unneeded services and ports, and assigning very strong passwords to the local administrator account.*

Work Factor *– Work factor is the level of effort required for an attacker to crack security controls, using a specific amount of resources, to achieve a specific objective. This objective may include unauthorized access to systems and data or it may be the decryption of ciphertext. One of the fundamental goals of implementing security controls is to increase the work factor to the point where the effort required to reach the objective is greater than the benefits gained.*

Just Enough Security

Defense in depth is a layered approach to applying controls. Figure 2-9 depicts the various layers that an organization should consider. Each of the physical, administrative, and technical categories on the stairway leading to Information Security should be assessed as part of an effective risk management effort.

Each layer is designed to provide support for the layers below it, and to prevent or detect the advance of an attacker to his objective. The layers work in concert to delay and frustrate. It's the combination of the right policies, processes, and controls at the appropriate layers that provide a secure processing environment.

Part 2 of this book is dedicated to stepping through these layers.

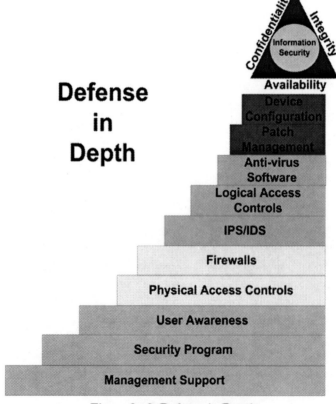

Figure 2 - 9: Defense in Depth

Recover

Recover is slightly different from prevent and detect. Although prevent and detect rely in part on process, recovery activities are all about

Information Security Primer

processes—processes that identify, contain, eradicate, and control. These processes are combined to form an organization's Incident Management Program. Figure 2-10 shows how the various processes relate to each other.

Once a security event is detected, the first step is to identify exactly what is occurring. For example, if a malware attack is suspected, what type of malware is it? What is the potential impact? How widespread is the infection? If an intruder has cracked a server, what data may be compromised? Is the intruder still accessing the information? The goal of the identify process is to correctly define what's happening, how it is happening, and the scope of the attack. This helps with the next process, contain.

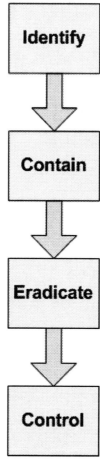

Figure 2 - 10: Four Processes of Incident Management

Once the attack parameters are defined, the impact on the business must be mitigated. This is called containment. If malware has infected a machine, disconnect the machine from the network. If the infection has spread to several computers on a floor at your corporate office, disconnect the floor. In the case of an intruder, remove her path to the target system. If the path is unclear, shut down the system. The goal of containment is to minimize the business impact of the attack. Beyond physical containment, communication to shareholders, employees, and customers may be necessary to properly convey information about the attack and to curtail rumors. In addition, regulatory requirements might mandate that you communicate to affected parties that a potential compromise of personal information has occurred.

Once the attack is contained, all threat agents must be eradicated. For malware, this means running vendor supplied removal programs, applying patches, or even re-imaging PC's. For other types of attacks, notification of law enforcement or the termination of one or more employees may be appropriate. The Incident Management process should include a list of actions to take based on the type of attack identified. The purpose of eradication is to remove all remnants of the attack from your network.

The control or management process wraps up the management of an incident by answering four questions:

1. What happened?
2. What was the cause?
3. What controls failed or were missing?
4. What steps can be taken to
    a. prevent similar future incidents,
    b. detect similar future incidents faster, and
    c. recover from similar future incidents more quickly?

The primary tool of the control process is the After Action Review (AAR). The AAR, explained in detail in Chapter 9, is a meeting held after the attack is contained and eradicated. The attendees at the meeting include all individuals who participated in dealing with the security incident. The input to the meeting is the open and frank observations of the attendees. Answers to the four questions listed above are the output.

Once the results of the AAR are fully documented, the answers to the elements in question 4 are converted into an action plan or, in some cases, one or more project plans. What controls are necessary, the types of modifications to be made to existing controls, and the resources to be applied to remediation efforts should be based on an effective Risk Management process.

CHAPTER SUMMARY

In this chapter, I've presented a high-level view of Information Security. But although Information Security is a very wide field of study, it isn't necessary to understand all the subtleties in every security domain to provide effective security for your organization. The basic understanding of security required to move to Part II in this book was presented in this chapter. Included were the definition of Information Security and the three levels of security controls: preventive, detective, and recovery. We also explored the value of using diversity in design and defense in depth to apply those controls. Finally, we took a very brief look at how to manage a security incident if prevention or early detection controls fail.

We covered all the elements in Figure 2-5 except one—Risk Management. As I wrote in this chapter, risk management is the process in a solid security program that helps managers make informed decisions about what and how many resources should be expended to prevent and detect specific threat agents. This is an important and often overlooked area of Information Security. I highly recommend you spend some time in Chapter 3—enough time to understand the importance of risk management and how to implement a risk management program in your organization.

CHAPTER 3
RISK MANAGEMENT PRIMER

Upon completion of this chapter, you will be able to:

1. Explain the importance of employing *risk management* within your organization
2. Discuss the Risk Formula, *Risk = Threats* x *Vulnerabilities* x *Business Impact*
3. Determine the value of an *information asset*
4. Explain the components of a *risk assessment*
5. Conduct a simple *risk assessment*
6. Select *reasonable and appropriate safeguards* for specific threat-vulnerability pairs
7. *Measure* the effectiveness of your Risk Management efforts

RISK

We encounter risk every day. There's the risk associated with making a financial investment. There's the risk of hiring the wrong person to manage key operations. Risk can also involve something as simple as making a left turn at a busy intersection. Although each of these situations occurs within a unique context, they all have something in common; they can all be generally defined by a very simple formula.

Risk = Threats x Vulnerabilities x Impact

A closer look at the formula shows that the elements of threats, vulnerabilities, and impact are multiplied together to arrive at risk. So reducing any one of the three will significantly reduce risk. Let's examine our left turn.

While making our turn, oncoming traffic is a threat. Vulnerabilities that increase your risk might include visibility restrictions on you or the other drivers, not wearing your seatbelt, or operating a vehicle with a low impact safety rating. Financial or personal impact due to an accident increases with factors such as having family members in the car or the size of your insurance deductible.

The lack of oncoming traffic reduces the threat level to zero, thereby eliminating risk. Wearing your seatbelt or ensuring you use your headlights when appropriate reduces your vulnerabilities. Finally, reducing your deductible might lower financial impact. This is a very simple day-to-day example of how to assess and reduce or eliminate risk. But how do the elements of risk apply to information assets?

Information assets include information, in any form, upon which an organization places value. These assets may include databases, programs, and the components of your network as well as information on paper. Also included is the most important asset your business possesses—your people. A cracker attempting to access your financial data, a virus that may corrupt production information, and a hurricane are all examples of threats against these assets.

A **threat** is any technological, natural, or man-made cause of harm to an information asset. **Vulnerabilities** are weaknesses in the security of an information system that might be exploited by a threat. Examples include programs that have not had security patches applied, unlocked computer rooms, and weak or widely known passwords. A threat

Risk Management Primer

exploiting a vulnerability resulting in the partial or total loss of one or more business assets constitutes business **impact.**

Eliminating threats to information resources is difficult, if not impossible. We have very little control over the actions of crackers, malicious code moving across the Internet, or the unintentional destruction of an asset by a trusted employee. Similarly, the ability to reduce impact to zero would most likely mean that the assets involved had little or no value to begin with. This leaves vulnerabilities. Eliminating or minimizing vulnerabilities is usually the most effective way to maintain acceptable levels of risk to the confidentiality, integrity, and availability of your information assets.

RISK MANAGEMENT

Risk management is about identifying risk, assessing the impact on your business if a security incident occurs, and making the right financial decision about how to deal with the results of your assessment. It also includes the implementation of a program to continually measure and assess the effectiveness of existing safeguards in protecting your critical assets.

Managing risk is not a one-time activity; it's an ongoing process. Figure 3-1 depicts the JES Risk Management Cycle.

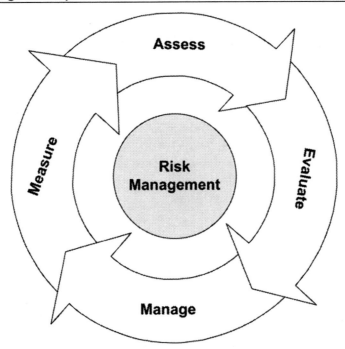

Figure 3 - 1: JES Risk Management Cycle

The first step in the cycle is to conduct a risk **assessment**. A risk assessment, explained in detail later in this chapter, identifies the following:

1. Critical information assets
2. Potential threats against critical assets
3. Critical asset vulnerabilities
4. Risks associated with each critical information asset

The risk assessment is followed by an **evaluation** of the risks identified during the assessment. The first step in the evaluation stage is the prioritization of the various risks. When ordering the list of risks, the risks with the highest risk scores have the highest priority. The final evaluation activity is identifying safeguards, and associated costs, to reduce the effects of risk exposure to the organization.

Next, management selects and implements the appropriate approach to **managing** each risk. Risk management is based on the premise that risk can probably never be reduced to zero. The cost is too high. Rather, management's goal should be to address specific risks in one of the following ways:

1. Reject
2. Accept
3. Transfer
4. Mitigate

Reject

Rejecting risk is never a good approach. By rejecting risk, a manager is saying that he doesn't believe the risk exists, so he does nothing. This is the head-in-the-sand approach. Ignore it and maybe it will go away. This is a dangerous way to deal with potential negative impact on your business. If used as a general approach to dealing with security issues, rejection of risk exposes the organization to a host of threats.

Accept

Accepting risk may seem the same as rejecting risk, but it's actually much different. When a manager performs a security safeguard cost/benefit analysis, she might discover that the cost of mitigating the risk is greater than the impact on the business. In such cases, it's probably a better business decision to accept the risk and spend security dollars in more effective ways. I'll cover safeguards and related business value analyses later.

Transfer

Once a manager decides to deal with the risk, there are two approaches. He can either transfer or mitigate the risk. Transferring the risk is most often accomplished by purchasing insurance to cover some or all of the cost of a security incident.

Mitigate

Mitigation involves the implementation of security safeguards across people, process, and technology in a reasonable and appropriate manner such that risk is reduced to an acceptable level.

Finally, management must **measure** the effectiveness of the risk management decisions made in the previous phase. These metrics should be simple and meaningful. I'll show you how to build an effective set of metrics later in this chapter.

I'll now describe each of the four risk management steps in greater detail. If you haven't reviewed the *Erudio Sprockets, Inc.* information system description at the end of the Introduction, I recommend you do so now.

Figure I-2 is an example of an overall organization infrastructure. I'll use a subset of the ESI network to demonstrate Risk Management steps. This subset consists of the ESI Financial System, depicted in Figure 3-2, specifically Accounts Receivable (AR) payment posting.

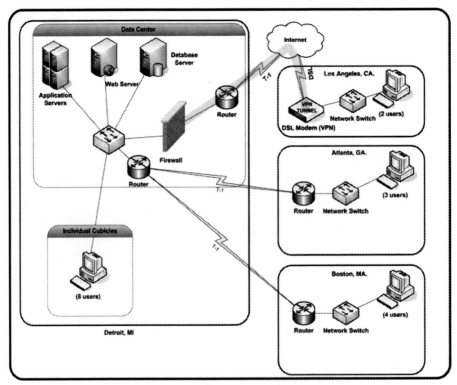

Figure 3 - 2: ESI Finance Infrastructure

The Risk Assessment Process

Before we dig into the Risk Assessment process, it's important that you understand the language of Risk Management. Please make sure you understand the following terms before continuing.

Security Event – A security event occurs when a threat exploits a vulnerability resulting in a business impact.

Exposure – Incurring losses due to a security event.

EF (Exposure Factor) – EF represents the extent to which an organization will incur a loss due to the compromise of an information asset. EF is expressed as a percentage. For example, if the value of an asset is $100,000, and the EF is 10%, the expected loss from a single event is $10,000. This is known as Single Loss Expectancy.

SLE (Single Loss Expectancy) – The SLE is the expected loss to an organization if a specific security exposure occurs. It is expressed as

SLE = (Asset Value x EF)

ARO (Annual Rate of Occurrence) – This is the number of times per year an organization expects a specific security exposure to occur. For example, if an organization's network is compromised by a virus about once every four years, the ARO of this threat is .25. If a virus event occurs three times per year, the ARO is 3. This is another way of expressing *Probability of Occurrence*.

ALE (Annual Loss Expectancy) – ALE is the annual cost an organization expects to incur due to a security event. It is expressed as

ALE = (SLE x ARO)

Probability of Occurrence – The likelihood that a threat/vulnerability pair will cause an exposure is the probability of occurrence.

Armed with the proper vocabulary, we're ready to take a look at the Risk Assessment Process.

The process

Figure 3-3 depicts the flow of a risk assessment, including the inputs and outputs of each process step. There are two approaches to following this process. The first results in a **qualitative** assessment. A qualitative assessment uses the experience and insights of employees to determine the level of risk associated with various system threats and vulnerabilities. Instead of arriving at a dollar amount to represent risk, the results of the assessment are levels of risk in terms of Low, Medium, or High. The second method is **quantitative.** This method uses actual dollar amounts to calculate a statistical, cost-based risk.

The first three steps in a risk assessment are essentially the same regardless of the method used. But the final three steps may differ significantly between qualitative and quantitative approaches. As we work through an abbreviated risk assessment for the ESI Financial system, we'll go down both qualitative and quantitative paths.

Risk Management Primer

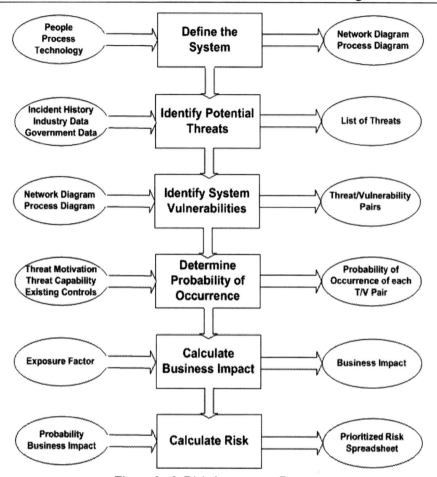

Figure 3 - 3: Risk Assessment Process

Define the system

To assess system vulnerabilities, we must understand the system end to end. In other words, we must know what hardware and software components are required to deliver the required information services to our employees or customers. In addition, we need to know how critical this system is to the effective operation of the business. This information will help when calculating business impact and when deciding where security dollars should be spent.

The core of the ESI finance system is a web-enabled application. In other words, both local and remote users access the application through web browsers. Examples of web browsers include Microsoft Internet

Explorer and Mozilla's Firefox. Figure 3-4 shows how connections are made and how data flows between the primary application components.

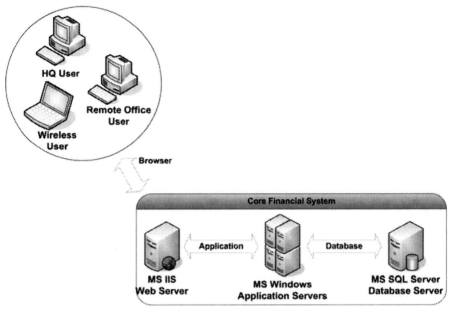

Figure 3 - 4: ESI Core Finance System

Using a web browser, each user connects to the Web Server. The Web Server establishes a connection to one of the Application Servers where the finance application actually runs. The finance application connects to the Database Server to store and retrieve financial information. This is a simplistic view of how the system works, but it's adequate for our purposes.

The workstations and servers shown in Figure 3-4 communicate with each other through the use of switches, routers, firewalls, and access points, as depicted in Figure 3-2. All these components, and the flow of information between them, must be understood in order to identify system vulnerabilities. It's also necessary to understand how each of the hardware components is configured. For example, we need to know what kind of information is allowed through the firewall into the ESI internal network. Knowing the kinds of information flows permitted, we can assess potential threats and vulnerabilities. Finally, it's important to know the version and patch levels of each operating system and application used in delivering the finance system. These topics will be covered in greater detail in later chapters.

In addition to infrastructure definitions, we must also understand the manual processes associated with the system. These processes include:

1. How individuals interact with the system
2. How duties are segregated
3. Critical processes and how the failure of each process affects the business and its customers, including

    a. Software failure – Failure of the software to perform as expected
    b. Process failure – Outcomes produced that do not meet customer expectations
    c. Hardware failure – Failure of an infrastructure component that interrupts system processing
    d. Human failure – The loss of a key individual, or intentional or unintentional harm caused by human interaction with the system

The outputs of this Risk Assessment step include a network diagram and a process diagram. Figures 3-2 and 3-4 are examples of simple network diagrams.

It's important not to get too hung up on the network diagram. I've seen some that could be mistaken for murals. Just make sure you have enough information to understand how the system works, how information flows, and how people interact. This is a good start and much more than most businesses have completed.

A process diagram shows how manual and automated activities produce results from the system. There are many methodologies you can use, or you can make up your own. As with the network diagram, the only requirement is to show a complete and accurate picture of each system process. Each system usually requires more than one process to use it effectively. Examples of finance processes include,

1. Entering journal entries
2. Entering and posting invoices
3. Entering and posting AR payments

Just Enough Security

4. Posting transactions to General Ledger (GL)
5. Month-end close

Figure 3-5 is one way to diagram a process. Note that the process diagram includes both manual and computer centered activities.

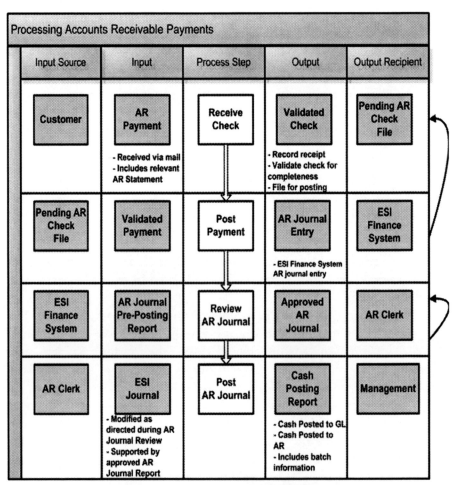

Figure 3 - 5: ESI AR Check Posting Process

The middle *Process Step* column depicts the process as it is now. Columns on either side of the process steps define the inputs and outputs associated with each step. Some inputs and outputs, such as *Validated Check*, define input/output attributes that are critical to producing a quality overall process output. The arrows to the right represent repetitive steps. The cycle of receiving a check followed by posting the check can occur many times before moving to the final two process steps. Also, the *Review AR Journal* step is repeated until the journal entries to be posted are corrected and approved.

To complete the documentation of our process, it's necessary to map the process steps to employees. Understanding how the process moves through the AR team helps us identify possible security risks, such as lack of segregation of duties. Table 3-1 lists the employee role responsible for each step in the ESI AR Check Posting process.

Process Step	Responsible Role
Receive Check	AR Clerk
Post Check	AR Clerk
Review AR Journal	AR Clerk
Post AR Journal	AR Clerk

Table 3 - 1: Assigned Roles in ESI AR Check Posting Process

Note the lack of segregation of duties. The AR Clerk performs all tasks associated with receiving, validating, and posting payments.

Identify potential threats

Potentially, a system is exposed to many natural, man-made, and human threats. Table 3-2 is a fairly comprehensive threat list. It doesn't contain all possible threats, nor do all the threats in the list necessarily apply to your organization. Each organization should choose the threats that are most reasonable—given its physical location and workforce makeup.

The threat type will help determine how to best protect against potential incidents. For example, certain man-made threats might be mitigated through training and continuous awareness activities. Natural threats might be mitigated by properly locating a facility or through the use of barriers or other structural safeguards.

Some threats may fall into multiple types. There's no right or wrong type assignment. Instead, it's right to think through the opportunities for threats to impact your business and wrong to fail to look at all relevant possibilities.

I've selected five common threats to use during our risk assessment. These are listed in Figure 3-6, which is an extract of a risk assessment

Just Enough Security

tool we'll be using throughout our finance system assessment. The next assessment step is the identification of system vulnerabilities.

Threat	Threat Types		
	Man-made	Natural	Tech.
Fire	X	X	
Flood		X	
Storms		X	
Explosions	X		
Bombings	X		
Earthquake		X	
Extreme Temperatures		X	
Building Collapse	X	X	
Power Failure	X	X	
Power Fluctuations	X		
Hardware Failure			X
Software Failure			X
Terrorist Attack	X		
Espionage/Sabotage	X		
Civil Disturbance	X		
Strikes	X		
High Humidity	X	X	
Communication Failure	X		
Broken Pipes	X		
Unhappy Employees	X		
Employee Error	X		
Vandalism	X		
Theft	X		
Malicious Code	X		
Fraud	X		
Embezzlement	X		
Intruders	X		
Unintentional Acts	X		
Unauthorized Access	X		
Poor or Undocumented Process			X
Improper Operations			X
Incorrect or Improper Hardware Configuration			X
Incorrect or Improper Software Configuration			X
Poor Change Management Controls			X
Data Entry Errors	X		X
Electromagnetic Emanations	X		X

Table 3 - 2: Potential Threats

Risk Management Primer

System: ESI Finance System Assessor: IS Manager	
Threat	**Vulnerability**
Fire	
Power Failure	
Malicious Code	
Employee Error	
Incorrect or Improper Hardware Configuration	

Figure 3 - 6: Threat List

Identify system vulnerabilities

A threat hasn't much of a chance to play havoc with your business if no vulnerabilities to that threat exist. In a perfect world, you could afford to eliminate all vulnerabilities. In the real world, the cost associated with removing all vulnerabilities is usually much too high to make good business sense. Although it's not usually possible to completely eliminate vulnerabilities, it's important to identify and prioritize existing vulnerabilities in order to apply security dollars effectively.

There's a many-to-many relationship between threats and vulnerabilities; one threat may potentially exploit one or more vulnerabilities, and one vulnerability may be exploited by one or more threats. Again, you should identify those threat-vulnerability pairs that are most relevant to your situation. Figure 3-7 expands our threat list to include vulnerabilities. I'm keeping it simple; your list of threat-vulnerability pairs will probably be much longer.

How we approach the remaining risk assessment steps depends on the type of assessment we're conducting. You may remember that the two assessment types are qualitative and quantitative. To demonstrate how the assessments differ, I've provided examples of both as we move through the next three process steps.

Just Enough Security

System: ESI Finance System Assessor: IS Manager	
Threat	**Vulnerability**
Fire	Water-based, standard office sprinkler system
Power Failure	The alternate power source provides only 60 minutes of backup power
Downloading Malicious Code	No centralized monitoring or update solution exists
Embezzlement/Fraud	Lack of Segregation of Duties
Implementation into Production of Incorrect or Improper Hardware Configuration	Lack of testing/change management processes

Figure 3 - 7: Threat-Vulnerability Pairs

Determine probability of occurrence, business impact, and risk

From a qualitative perspective, the probability of occurrence is an educated guess about the probability that an identified threat will attempt to exploit a specific vulnerability. It's expressed as a value from .01 to 1.0, with 1.0 representing 100% probability of occurrence. Probability scores are affected by things like the location of the business or the means, motivation, and opportunity of human threats.

Figure 3-8 depicts the first six columns of the spreadsheet I use for qualitative risk assessments.

Risk Management Primer

System: ESI Finance System			Date: January 25, 2005		
Assessor: IS Manager					

Threat	Vulnerability	Prob	Business Impact	Impact	Risk
Downloading Malicious Code	No centralized monitoring or update solution exists	1.00	May result in loss of production tracking, order processing, or completion of payroll.	75	75.00
Power Failure	The alternate power source provides only 60 minutes of backup power	1.00	May result in loss of production tracking, order processing, or completion of payroll.	50	50.00
Embezzlement/Fraud	Lack of Segregation of Duties	0.25	May result in the moderate loss of assets or resources.	75	18.75
Implementation into Production of Incorrect or Improper Hardware Configuration	Lack of testing/change management processes	0.15	May result in the moderate loss of revenue or productivity.	85	12.75
Fire	Water-based, standard office sprinkler system.	0.05	Potential Destruction of all systems in the data center	80	4.00

Figure 3 - 8: Qualitative Risk Assessment

Suggested Probabilities	
Threat Likelihood	Probability
High	.51 to 1.00
Medium	.11 to .50
Low	.01 to .10

Table 3 - 3: Suggested Probability Ranges

The probability table I used for this assessment is shown in Table 3-3. The probabilities of occurrence in our example vary widely, from low (.01) to absolute certainty (1.00). But a high probability of occurrence does not necessarily translate to a high level of risk, nor does a low probability mean that an organization has nothing to worry about. To arrive at the level of risk caused by a threat-vulnerability pair, we must also factor in business impact. Business impact might include:

1. Cost of loss of assets or resources
2. Violation, harm, or hindrance to an organization's mission, reputation, or interest
3. Human death or injury

Table 3-4 suggests three levels of business impact.

Impact	Impact Definition (Stoneburner, Goguen, & Feringa, 2002)
High **100**	1. May result in significant financial loss of critical assets or resources. 2. May seriously violate, harm, or impede the organization's mission or reputation. 3. May result in grievous human injury or death.
Medium **50**	1. May result in moderate loss of assets or resources. 2. May violate, harm, or impede the organization's mission or reputation. 3. May result in human injury.
Low **10**	1. May result in the loss of some assets or resources. 2. May noticeably affect an organization's mission or reputation.

Table 3 - 4: Suggested Levels of Business Impact

The business impact score is located on a continuum between 0 and 100. In a qualitative analysis, the score selected is based on employee experience, training, and an educated guess. The business impact score should be arrived at through interviews and surveys involving all key stakeholders. The effectiveness of existing safeguards must also be included in the impact scoring process. For example, if there was an appropriate fire suppression system in place at ESI, the business impact resulting from a fire would fall well below 80. It's important to remember that each vulnerability may have more than one safeguard. An impact description is also included in our risk assessment spreadsheet.

The risk score for each threat-vulnerability pair is calculated by multiplying the probability of occurrence by the impact score. Looking at Figure 3-8, we see that both probability and impact play major roles in arriving at risk. In our fire example, the impact score of 80 is significantly mitigated by a probability of .05. The risk presented by a power failure is in the high medium range, even though the impact score is much less than that of the fire threat. Table 3-5 provides some guidelines for dealing with various risk scores.

Risk	Risk Description and Necessary Actions (Stoneburner, Goguen, & Feringa, 2002)
High 51 to 100	If an observation or finding is evaluated as a high risk, there is a strong need for corrective measures. An existing system may continue to operate, but a corrective action plan must be put in place as soon as possible.
Medium 11 to 50	If an observation is rated as medium risk, corrective actions are needed and a plan must be developed to incorporate these actions within a reasonable period of time.
Low 1 to 10	If an observation is described as low risk, the system's data owner must determine whether corrective actions are still required or decide to accept the risk.

Table 3 - 5: Risk Guidelines

Once you calculate the risk scores, sort the spreadsheet by risk, from highest to lowest. Your best return on security investment results from applying your security resources to the implementation of safeguards to defend against the threat-vulnerabilities with the highest risk. This is the focus of the Evaluate step of the Risk Management process. Before we proceed to evaluating possible safeguards, however, we need to see how this assessment would look if using the quantitative method.

When performing a quantitative assessment, we start with a calculation of asset value. Costs that contribute to asset value include:

1. **Product Cost** – The purchase price of each system component.

2. **Professional Services Cost** – The cost of engaging outside assistance to install, configure, and test each system component.

3. **Internal Resources Setup Costs** – This cost category represents the costs associated with the internal human resources you must engage to replace each system component.

4. **Confidentiality** – The cost associated with the loss of information confidentiality. An example might be fines due to regulatory issues. Potential litigation initiated by customers

whose personal information is compromised will also affect cost in this category.

5. **Integrity** – The cost incurred when there is a loss of faith in the accuracy of information assets. Fines related to Sarbanes-Oxley or loss of shareholder confidence are examples of costs in this category. This category also includes losses due to incorrect data in financial and customer facing systems.

6. **Availability** – Losses related to idle employees or idle manufacturing processes are good examples of costs associated with availability.

Figure 3-9 is a business impact calculator I use for risk assessments. Each hardware and software component is listed under each threat-vulnerability pair. In our example, there's only one vulnerability per threat. So I listed threats only. The *Cost of Replacement* categories are reasonably easy to obtain. Invoices and purchase orders are a good starting point for product and professional services. If you don't have these documents, your vendors should be able to provide replacement costs.

Most companies have some idea of the hourly cost of each employee. Remember to include taxes and benefits. This information is used to calculate the cost of having internal resources participate in recovery operations.

To arrive at the value of a component, the costs of replacement are added to the costs associated with confidentiality, integrity, and availability. These values are totaled to arrive at the overall value of the system.

Once the system value is known, it's multiplied by an exposure factor. The exposure factor is calculated by taking into account the following:

1. The motivation of the threat
2. The impact on the asset if there were no safeguards in place
3. The quality and effectiveness of the safeguards in place at the time of the assessment

Risk Management Primer

Business Impact (SLE) Calculation									
	Cost of Replacement			Costs Associated with Loss of					
Asset Description	Product Cost	Professional Services Cost	Internal Resources Setup Costs	Confidentiality	Integrity	Availability	Asset Value	Exposure Factor (%)	Single Loss Expectancy
Data Center Fire									
Application Servers	20,000	10,000	2,500	0	0	96,000	128,500		
Web Server	5,000	2,500	1,000	0	0		8,500		
Database Server	45,000	2,500	1,000	0	32,000		80,500		
Ethernet Switch	7,500	1,500	1,000	0	0		10,000		
Firewall	5,000	1,500	500	0	0		7,000		
Router (2)	15,000	3,000	1,000	0	0		19,000		
Information	750,000	25,000	35,000	0	0		810,000		
							1,063,500	80.00% $	850,800
Power Failure									
Application Servers	20,000	10,000	2,500	0	0	16,000	48,500		
Web Server	5,000	2,500	1,000	0	0		8,500		
Database Server	45,000	2,500	1,000	0	0		48,500		
Ethernet Switch	7,500	1,500	1,000	0	0		10,000		
Firewall	5,000	1,500	500	0	0		7,000		
Router (2)	15,000	3,000	1,000	0	0		19,000		
Information	750,000	25,000	35,000	0	0		810,000		
							951,500	5.00% $	47,575
Downloading Malicious Code									
Application Servers	20,000	10,000	2,500	0	0	16,000	48,500		
Web Server	5,000	2,500	1,000	0	0		8,500		
Database Server	45,000	2,500	1,000	0	0		48,500		
Ethernet Switch	7,500	1,500	1,000	0	0		10,000		
Firewall	5,000	1,500	500	0	0		7,000		
Router (2)	15,000	3,000	1,000	0	0		19,000		
Information	750,000	25,000	35,000	0	0		810,000		
							951,500	40.00% $	380,600
Embezzlement/Fraud									
Application Servers	20,000	10,000	2,500	0	0	0	32,500		
Web Server	5,000	2,500	1,000	0	0	0	8,500		
Database Server	45,000	2,500	1,000	0	0	0	48,500		
Ethernet Switch	7,500	1,500	1,000	0	0	0	10,000		
Firewall	5,000	1,500	500	0	0	0	7,000		
Router (2)	15,000	3,000	1,000	0	0	0	19,000		
Information	750,000	25,000	35,000	0	0	0	810,000		
							935,500	25.00% $	233,875
Incorrect Hardware/Software Configuration									
Application Servers	20,000	10,000	2,500	1,000	0	4,000	37,500		
Web Server	5,000	2,500	1,000	1,000	0	4,000	13,500		
Database Server	45,000	2,500	1,000	1,500	0	6,000	56,000		
Ethernet Switch	7,500	1,500	1,000	500	0	2,000	12,500		
Firewall	5,000	1,500	500	500	0	2,000	9,500		
Router (2)	15,000	3,000	1,000	1,000	0	4,000	24,000		
Information	750,000	25,000	35,000	50,000	50,000	150,000	1,060,000		
							1,213,000	1.00% $	12,130

Figure 3 - 9: SLE Calculation

System: ESI Finance System					
Assessor: IS Manager		Date:			

Threat	Vulnerability	ARO	Business Impact	SLE	ALE
Fire	No data center fire suppression system	0.05	Potential Destruction of all systems in the data center	850,800	42,540
Power Failure	The alternate power source provides only 60 minutes of backup power	2.00	May result in loss of production tracking, order processing, or completion of payroll.	47,575	95,150
Downloading Malicious Code	No centralized monitoring or update solution exists	0.50	May result in loss of production tracking, order processing, or completion of payroll.	380,600	190,300
Embezzlement/Fraud	Lack of Separation of Duties	0.10	May result in the moderate loss of assets or resources.	233,875	23,388
Implementation into Production of Incorrect or Improper Hardware Configuration	Lack of testing/change management processes	4.00	May result in the moderate loss of revenue or productivity.	12,130	48,520

Figure 3 - 10: ESI Quantitative Assessment

For example, a fire in the ESI data center may completely destroy the system if no safeguards exist—a 100% loss. However, the current safeguard of a standard sprinkler fire suppression system is expected to save a portion of the system, while a large part of it may suffer damage from water and smoke. In this sample assessment, I believe the current safeguard reduces business impact by only 20%. This results in an exposure factor of 80%. By multiplying the asset value by the exposure factor related to a fire, we arrive at a SLE of $850,000. The next step is to annualize the SLE.

Figure 3-10 shows the tool used to perform the final steps. It's similar to the tool used for our qualitative assessment. There are three significant differences. Probability is replaced by ARO, Impact is replaced by SLE, and Risk is replaced by ALE.

ESI management expects a fire every 20 years. This results in an ARO of .05. Multiplying this by the SLE of a fire, we arrive at an ALE of $42,540. The ALE represents the annual financial risk of the fire-suppression system threat-vulnerability pair. Note that even though fire has the highest loss expectancy per single occurrence, the annual financial risk associated with it is just above the lowest risk of Embezzlement/Fraud.

I made creating a quantitative assessment look easy; it isn't. Significant effort is required to come up with the costs and historical data necessary to calculate ARO and the EF. So why even bother with quantitative assessments?

Table 3-6 shows the advantages and disadvantages of each assessment approach. It's clear there are benefits to using each approach. But neither provides a complete picture of the risks your organization faces. That's why I recommend using both. Wait. Don't panic. It's not that bad.

How you use these methodologies is up to you. One approach is to perform a qualitative assessment to determine the perceived level of risk associated with each system. This is followed by a quantitative assessment that provides enough information to demonstrate ROSI. This is the approach we'll take as we proceed through the ESI assessment evaluation. Your approach can be as creative as you are—and it depends in part on how much cost information is readily available.

Now that our assessment is complete, we move to the next phase of our Risk Management Cycle—evaluate.

	Advantages	Disadvantages
Quantitative	The value of information is expressed in terms of dollars with supporting information The risk values are derived and shown in a format familiar to decision makers Much easier to show a Return on Security Investment (ROSI)	A purely quantitative risk assessment is not possible; quantitative measures must be applied to qualitative components A large amount of information must be gathered and assessed to arrive at the values used Although the results may be less ambiguous, the use of actual dollar amounts may give the appearance of an accuracy that does not actually exist
Qualitative	Simple and easily understood and implemented Provides a quick picture of areas of risk that should be addressed	Subjective in both process and measurements Cannot provide a clear ROSI

Table 3 - 6: Quantitative vs. Qualitative

Evaluate

To evaluate the ESI risk assessment, we'll first look at the qualitative analysis we performed in the Assessment phase. Figure 3-11 shows the ESI qualitative assessment sorted by risk value. The threat-vulnerability pair with the largest risk value is *Downloading Malicious Code*. For our evaluation example, we'll focus only on this pair.

System: ESI Finance System			Date: January 25, 2005		
Assessor: IS Manager					
Threat	Vulnerability	Prob	Business Impact	Impact	Risk
Downloading Malicious Code	No centralized monitoring or update solution exists	1.00	May result in loss of production tracking, order processing, or completion of payroll.	75	75.00
Power Failure	The alternate power source provides only 60 minutes of backup power	1.00	May result in loss of production tracking, order processing, or completion of payroll.	50	50.00
Embezzlement/Fraud	Lack of Segregation of Duties	0.25	May result in the moderate loss of assets or resources.	75	18.75
Implementation into Production of Incorrect or Improper Hardware Configuration	Lack of testing/change management processes	0.15	May result in the moderate loss of revenue or productivity.	85	12.75
Fire	Water-based, standard office sprinkler system.	0.05	Potential Destruction of all systems in the data center	80	4.00

Figure 3 - 11: Sorted Qualitative Assessment

We listed the vulnerability in this case as *no centralized monitoring or update solution exists*. This results in workstations with either no protection or protection that's not up-to-date. It also means that the support team doesn't know malware is on its network until it begins to significantly impact system availability. Our objective in defining a safeguard is to address these issues. Meeting with ESI management, it was decided to implement a centralized, automated management system that performs the following tasks:

1. Checks to ensure each workstation and server on the network is running the approved anti-virus software
2. Checks to ensure that the virus identification files are up-to-date on each workstation and server
3. Generates a daily report that identifies infected systems

Risk Management Primer

After evaluating several solutions, ESI tentatively selected a solution with a product cost of $75,000.

Once the safeguard is identified, a cost-benefit analysis is conducted to determine whether the annual cost of the safeguard exceeds annual exposure. Experiencing an annual return on security investment (ROSI) depends on the intelligent application of safeguards. Figure 3-12 shows an annual cost of ownership calculation for the selected solution.

Annual TCO Calculation Cost Category	Cost
Implementation Costs	
Product Purchase	75,000
Network Upgrades	40,000
Professional Services Implementation	5,000
Training	2,500
Total Implementation Cost	**122,500**
Annual Recurring Costs	
Maintenance	15,000
System Management	20,000
Annual Recurring Cost	**35,000**
Annual Cost of Ownership	
Implementation cost annualized over estimated solution life (5 Years)	24,500
Annual Recurring Cost	35,000
Total Annual Cost over 5 Years	**59,500**

Figure 3 - 12: Annual TCO Calculation

Having already calculated the original ALE for this threat-vulnerability pair as $380,600, we're ready to begin our ROSI calculation. The first step is to estimate the reduction in ALE if the safeguard is implemented. Any reduction in the ALE is the annual cost reduction realized by our security investment. First, let's take a look at the SLE.

Management believes the EF is reduced from 40% to 10%. The Support Team's ability to quickly identify and deal with infections before they result in a serious exposure is significantly improved. Multiplying the asset value by the new EF results in a SLE of $95,150.

Assessing the impact of the safeguard's protection against an event occurring, we dropped the ARO to .50 representing a probability of occurrence of once every two years. Remember, we define ARO as the number of times in a single year that a threat takes advantage of a vulnerability resulting in an exposure. Remaining vulnerabilities prevent further reduction of the ARO. For example, malware signature updates are not released for customer use until well after the malware hits the Internet. Multiplying the SLE of $95,150 by the new ARO of .50 results in an ALE of $47,575.

To determine the annual ROSI of an investment in this solution, we subtract the annual cost from the change in ALE.

ROSI = (Old ALE – New ALE) - Annual Cost of Safeguard
ROSI = (380,600 - 47,575) - 59,500
ROSI = $273,525

In this case, there is a positive and rather substantial annual ROSI.

In an actual assessment evaluation, the assessment team will perform these evaluation steps on each threat-vulnerability pair with a higher than acceptable risk level. So does this mean that we go ahead and make an investment wherever the ROSI is greater than zero? This is determined in the next phase of Risk Management.

Manage

Figure 3-13 shows both the quantitative and qualitative results of our evaluation of all threat-vulnerability pairs from Figure 3-10, sorted by ROSI.

Risk Management Primer

Threat	Vulnerability	Safeguard	ROSI	ALE	Risk
Downloading Malicious Code	No centralized monitoring or update solution exists	Implementation of centralized monitoring and update system	$ 273,525	$ 380,600	75.00
Implementation into Production of Incorrect or Improper Hardware Configuration	Lack of testing/change management processes	Development and implementation of a change management process	$ 38,500	$ 48,520	12.75
Fire	No data center fire suppression system	Implementation of an Inergen-based system	$ 32,500	$ 42,540	4.00
Power Failure	The alternate power source provides only 60 minutes of backup power	Implementation of a diesel powered generator	$ 25,000	$ 95,150	50.00
Embezzlement/ Fraud	Lack of Separation of Duties	Rewrite processes to change responsibilities	$ 21,000	$ 23,388	18.75

Figure 3 - 13: ESI Assessment Results

If we were to base our security spending decisions strictly on ROSI, we'd begin with the implementation of a centralized malware monitoring and updating system followed by the development of a Change Management process. But this is where management should use both quantitative and qualitative results to decide on the best use of its security dollars.

Quantitative risk assessments can be poor tools for evaluating intangible business impact. This is where qualitative assessments add real value. Intangible impact includes:

1. Serious injury or death
2. Diminished company reputation
3. Long term impact of a significant delivery interruption
4. Loss of investor confidence
5. Loss of competitive advantage due to theft or loss of intellectual property

Each organization must identify intangible risks to its continued operation.

If we properly assessed both tangible and intangible business impact during our qualitative assessment, the numbers in the *Risk* column should be carefully considered in our spending decisions. These numbers represent management's

1. knowledge of the business,
2. knowledge of its customers and investors,
3. knowledge of the industry in which it operates, and
4. past experience with similar security events.

This knowledge and experience shouldn't be dismissed when assessing risk. ESI management believes that the qualitative risk number is a more accurate measure of overall security risk. They will use the quantitative results, and the ROSI, to help determine whether the recommended safeguards are cost effective. Due to budgetary constraints, they decided to mitigate the power and malware risks by implementing a diesel-powered generator as well as a centralized malware prevention and detection system. They will accept the other risks until the related implementation costs are included in future budgets.

Management of security safeguards go beyond implementation. Regular testing and maintenance must be made part of normal operations. Over time, ESI should measure the effectiveness of implemented safeguards. This is the topic of the next section.

Measure

As most managers know, you can't improve what you don't measure. Measuring the benefits to your business from security activities is a key component to managing risk. There are three metrics I recommend you use to measure the effectiveness of your risk management efforts.

1. The rise or fall in the frequency of security events
2. The rise or fall in the magnitude of the exposure of specific security events
3. The ratio of the cost of security activities to the cost of security events (either in general or by system)

There may be others you want to use. Just remember that you should only track those metrics that measure the objectives you are trying to reach. Don't fall into the trap of making security metric management a career path within your organization.

The rise or fall in the frequency of security events.

Although you won't eliminate all vulnerabilities, you should be able to lower the number of successful exploits associated with threat-vulnerability pairs. This should be relatively easy to track. If you have an Incident Management Process in place, recording metric related information for each event is just another step in the process. The frequency measured should match the probability unit of measure in your assessments. Frequency of occurrence is usually reported as the number of occurrences in one year. This matches the ARO and probability factors in quantitative and qualitative assessment methods.

The rise or fall in the magnitude of the exposure of specific security events.

When an event does occur, it usually has an impact on the business. One of the key objectives in Risk Management is mitigating exposure due to security events. In order to properly employ this metric, costs associated with security events must be tracked. Tracking should begin with a baseline cost. The baseline costs can either be the average exposure from a security event in the past, or the cost of the last occurrence of the event. Again, calculating the cost of a security event should be part of your Incident Management Process.

The ratio of the cost of security activities to the cost of security events.

This ratio helps to measure the effectiveness of your Risk Management Program as well as your overall Security Program. If you follow the ROSI guidelines presented earlier, you'll be positioned to improve the cost effectiveness of these programs. The accuracy of this cost ratio depends on two factors. First, you must have a good understanding of the cost of your organization's security activities. Second, you must track costs associated with security events. We've discussed security event costs in other parts of this chapter. Let's take a look at calculating security costs.

Basic security activities include:

1. Identity Management
    a. Managing accounts
    b. Access controls
2. Network/system monitoring and incident response
3. Policy and process development and oversight
4. Network/system vulnerability management
5. Risk assessments on both proposed and existing systems

There are hardware, software, and people costs associated with each activity on this list. The sum of these costs is the total cost for your security efforts. You can track these costs for your enterprise or for individual systems. I recommend you do both. You should track your enterprise security cost to measure your overall effectiveness. You should track the security costs associated with each critical business system to measure your efforts to protect your most valuable information assets.

Once you have the costs, calculate the value expressed by the ratio. For example, if the annual cost of protecting the ESI Financial system is $15,000 and the average loss due to security incidents is $50,000, the ratio value is,

$$\text{Effectiveness Value} = \frac{\text{Cost of Security Activities}}{\text{Cost of Security Events}}$$

$$\text{Effectiveness Value} = \frac{15{,}000}{50{,}000}$$

$$\text{Effectiveness Value} = .3$$

Risk Management Primer

This number in isolation means very little. However, when used as a baseline to measure how information asset protection is impacted by the rise or fall of security costs, it becomes very important. For instance, what would the Effectiveness Value of 1 mean a year after this baseline calculation was made because the Cost of Security Events dropped to $15,000? It might mean that your security activities have become more effective, so your costs remained the same while you provided even greater protection for your information assets. It could also mean that you were lucky. In any case, you want the annual percentage decrease in Cost of Security Events to exceed the annual percentage increase in Cost of Security Activities.

Although the Effectiveness Value is an important metric, it must be placed into the overall context of your security efforts before you can derive its appropriate meaning. I never said you wouldn't have to think in order to successfully manage risk.

I'd like to say one last thing about metrics. Metrics should not be used just to show management how well you're protecting its assets. You should also use them to measure how you're doing in your efforts to improve security effectiveness in every IS activity. We can always do better.

CHAPTER SUMMARY

Risk Management does not consist of a one-time process. It is a cyclical process consisting of risk assessment, evaluation of risk data, cost benefit analysis, and the implementation and monitoring of safeguards. It is through the execution of Risk Management activities that an organization is able to reduce and maintain risk at an acceptable level while realizing a return on security investment.

Qualitative and quantitative are two approaches to assessing risk. Used together, they provide a picture of an organization's risk that is based on both objective costs as well as subjective experience. Although using quantitative measures produces a "just about" ROSI, it does force managers and security consultants to think about cost vs. benefit.

Measuring the results of any safeguard implementation is crucial to improving Risk Management. It's important to understand whether the safeguards put in place affecting people, process, and technology improve information asset security.

Risk Management should drive most security activities. It helps determine the most effective use of security dollars.

Works Cited in Chapter 3

Stoneburner, G., Goguen, A, & Feringa, A. (2002). *Risk management guide for information technology systems (NIST Special Publication 800-30).* Retrieved April 1, 2005 from http://csrc.nist.gov/publications/nistpubs/800-30/sp800-30.pdf.

Part 2
JES

CHAPTER 4
THE JES SECURITY MODEL

The purpose of this chapter is to introduce and define the various layers of the JES Security Model. We also look at how the layers work together to provide a secure processing environment. In the chapters that follow, we take a more detailed look at the physical, technical, and administrative areas in each of the model layers.

Upon completion of this chapter, you'll be able to discuss:

1. The importance of a *layered approach* to protecting information resources
2. The layers of the *JES Model* and how they work together to provide a secure processing environment
3. How the JES model meets *confidentiality, integrity,* and *availability* requirements

JUST ENOUGH SECURITY

The Just Enough Security (JES) model is based on the premise that it takes *layers* of controls to effectively protect information assets. Also known as "defense-in-depth," layered security takes on a variety of forms. The JES model is my take on a model for planning, implementing, and managing an organization's Information Security effort. Figure 4-1 depicts the JES approach.

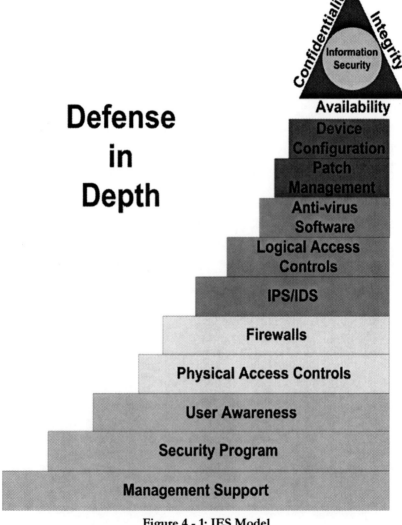

Figure 4 - 1: JES Model

The objective of layered security is to implement a variety of controls that work in concert to neutralize the efforts of a threat agent. A threat agent attempting to compromise the confidentiality, integrity, or availability of a system protected by a layered security environment passes through several different tests before reaching its target. These layers comprise administrative, physical, and technical safeguards. To be truly effective, this model must extend to all company owned devices, whether located on the company network, at home, or at a customer site.

Is it necessary to implement all layers to ensure security? Not necessarily. That's the point of JES. Which layers to implement, and to what extent, is a risk management decision. Chapter 3 defined a risk management process designed to help make informed decisions about how and when to apply controls. In the following sections and chapters, we look at each layer and how it fits into an overall security effort.

Management support

The foundation of any security program is management support. This support should be comprised, at a minimum, of effective policies, adequate budgets, and consistent enforcement. Efforts to change user behavior and to implement security measures carry no weight unless there is visible executive support from all levels of management. Visible support isn't just the hanging of a few posters around the lunch room. Effective support is evident in the project approval process, in the presence of a meaningful awareness program, and in how management deals with violations of security policy. It's reinforced in management and employee meetings, memos, and if appropriate, the annual report. In other words, management support of information security should be manifested as a part of the organization's culture.

Security program

An organization's security program defines and facilitates the security objectives of management. It consists of policies, procedures, standards, and guidelines. Policies are high-level statements of management's goals and objectives. They don't provide step-by-step directions to reach those goals and objectives; such directions are provided by procedures. A policy should consist of at least three elements:

1. Purpose
2. Scope
3. Compliance

The purpose element of a policy clearly explains the objectives it's intended to achieve. It should also reflect management's commitment to a secure enterprise. Scope describes all enterprise technology and activities affected by the policy. Finally, compliance defines consequences if the policy is not followed. It's the compliance piece—necessary to strongly encourage implementation—that's often missing from security policies.

Procedures are the administrative, physical, and technical recipes for producing a secure enterprise. They're derived from and support management policies. The step-by-step nature of procedures helps to ensure consistent compliance with security policy.

Along with procedures that support security policies, standards and guidelines form the security handbook of an organization. Standards are mandatory configurations and approaches to technology implementation. Guidelines assist implementers and managers with issues that are not specifically covered by standards; they aren't mandatory.

User awareness

Unless fully engaged in the company's security efforts, end-users can be an organization's greatest threat. Continuous awareness training is the best way to obtain end-user participation in a security program. Training should include:

1. Review of policies, standards, and guidelines
2. Implementation and configuration procedures
3. Password protection
4. How to deal with social engineering attacks
5. Proper protection of workstations
    a. Logging off before walking away from a device
    b. Use of systems by unauthorized users
    c. Elimination of potential **shoulder surfing** opportunities

The JES Security Model

6. Proper handling of PDAs, laptops, cell phones, etc.
7. Proper handling and disposition of media
   a. Backup tapes
   b. CD-ROM
   c. Floppy disks
   d. Other types of storage devices

> ### Key Terms
>
> ***Shoulder Surfing*** *– When a person looks over another's shoulder to see what keys she presses to enter her password, that's shoulder surfing. Shoulder surfing is a term used to describe any activity whereby a person watches a user perform some action that may result in the unauthorized and unintentional revelation of confidential information.*

User awareness should begin with new hire orientation. Existing employees should receive training at least annually. In addition to formal training, daily reminders should be everywhere in the workplace; posters and login messages are two good vehicles for reminder distribution. Managers should talk about security whenever appropriate during daily interaction with staff. Finally, first line managers must ensure that attention to security compliance is part of every operational task.

Physical access controls

The effectiveness of the security program is directly proportional to the effectiveness of the physical access controls surrounding information assets. Strong passwords, biometrics, and other logical access methods will not prevent the financial loss associated with the theft or physical destruction of critical business systems. Further, the level of effort applied to extracting information from secure devices within the normal business environment will probably fall far short of the effort applied in a cracker's basement.

Physical access controls include locked doors, cable locks, and security personnel. Only IS personnel whose day-to-day duties require it should have physical access to your data center. Also, educating users on the proper physical control of laptops, PDAs, and other mobile devices is an important factor in the prevention of information loss or compromise. This includes immediate notification of the appropriate manager if a portable device is lost or stolen.

Firewalls

The term "firewall" was traditionally used to describe a barrier that prevented fires from spreading. In a network, a firewall serves a similar purpose; it protects an organization's network from malware and other threat agents seeking to enter through connections to the Internet or other external networks. These connections are usually your network's weakest points. You can also place a firewall at the entry point into each subnet containing your most critical information. This helps prevent threat agents already on your network from spreading to your mission critical systems. So what is a network firewall?

A network firewall is a collection of programs that protect the resources of a private network. These programs can reside on a device designed to act as a firewall or on a server configured to act as a firewall. In either configuration, the firewall performs the same basic function; it inspects packets to determine if their content matches the criteria required to pass through to your internal or protected network. The types of packet inspection are covered in more detail in Chapter 6.

IPS/IDS

There are two primary types of Intrusion Protection Systems (IPS)—network and host. Network-based IPS systems protect the entire network or a network segment. Host-based IPS systems reside on and protect individual systems. The same is true of Intrusion Detection Systems (IDS). The primary difference between IPS and IDS is how each reacts to a potential attack. An IDS device reports the attack so that a human can react. Once an IPS device detects an attack, however, it can react automatically based on rules you set up. Most devices today combine IPS and IDS.

In an ideal environment, malicious code and unauthorized users are always denied access to critical systems. The protections in such an environment prevent authorized users from destabilizing their systems as well as the network. But who works in an ideal environment?

Host-based IPS is a layer of protection that attempts to "catch" activities not blocked by the lower layers lower of the JES model. These activities include but are not limited to the following:

1. Deleting files
2. Moving files
3. Copying files
4. Installing executable files
5. Registry modifications
6. Denial of service processes

Network IPS looks at network traffic, attempting to recognize attack patterns and behavior. Once a potential attack is identified, the IPS device can block traffic, shut down one or more services, or a number of other actions you define. This topic is covered in Chapter 7.

Logical access controls

Logical (technical) access controls include hardware or software components that prevent either unauthorized users from gaining access to information resources or authorized users from gaining access to information for which they have no data owner authorization. Logical controls include passwords, biometrics, and tokens. Regardless of the controls used, they should:

1. Have minimal impact on end-user productivity
2. Be reliable
3. Be effective with a ROI resulting from their initial and ongoing deployment costs

The way in which logical controls are implemented is just as important as which controls are selected. The following is a list of guidelines.

1. Relying on strong, easy to forget passwords may be a mistake for your organization. Strong passwords consist of upper case and lower case letters, numbers, and one or more special characters. Users often post strong passwords on their monitors or in other office locations that are less conspicuous but just as accessible. If you choose not to use strong passwords, make sure you look at **compensating controls**.

2. Establishing an effective account policy is crucial to a logical access control implementation. The policy should include the following:

   a. Automatic password expiration, usually 60 to 90 days
   b. A minimum password length, typically 6 to 8 characters
   c. Password history to ensure that a password is not reused when it expires
   d. A threshold of login attempts that when exceeded locks the user account, usually set at 3
   e. An effective lockout duration that deters **brute force attacks**

Finally, it is a good idea to combine password controls with another access control, such as biometrics. This is known as **two factor authentication**. If a password is compromised, the second control will help stop unauthorized use of system resources.

Key Terms

Compensating Control *– A compensating control is a process or technology that helps to make up for the lack of a primary control. For example, if your organization insists on assigning weak passwords to the local administrator accounts on your servers, a compensating control might be to implement much stricter controls on physical access to the data center. Since local accounts are used by someone actually standing at the server keyboard, imposing strong physical access restrictions can help reduce risk.*

Brute Force Attack *– There are two types of password attacks: dictionary and brute force. In a dictionary attack, a cracker compares a list of dictionary words to each password. This is the fastest method, since most users invariably use common words found in the dictionary for their passwords. If a dictionary attack fails, a cracker will often try a brute force attack. In this type of attack, every letter, number, and special character combination is compared against the list of passwords. If given enough time, a brute force attack can crack almost any password.*

Two Factor Authentication *– There are three principle approaches to* *authenticating a user to a system or network. These approaches include the use of something you know, something you are, or something you have. An example of something you know is your password. Your fingerprint is an example of something you are. A **token** is an example of something you have. The use of any two of the three approaches is called two factor authentication.*

Token *– A token is a physical object, usually about the size of a credit card, that identifies the person carrying it to a system or network. A token is typically used with a PIN.*

Antivirus software

Malicious code attacks are the most common type of penetration into a company's internal network. According to the CSI/FBI 2005 Computer Crime and Security Survey (www.gocsi.com), almost 33% of business losses related to security incidents are from virus attacks.

Why, when 96% of the nearly 700 respondents to the survey have an antivirus solution in place, did virus attacks retain the number one position? One explanation is the theory that target organizations often incorrectly report denial of service attacks as virus attacks. Another cause may be the failure on the part of many organizations to maintain current virus signature files. Hundreds of new worms and viruses are released each month. Without a consistent effort to keep antivirus solutions current and operational, every end user device in your network is a potential open door into your network. This is especially true of email systems.

Email has become one of the primary tools used by propagators of malware. Unsuspecting users opening attachments or distributing apparently harmless chain email can cause internal infections even on networks with a perfectly configured firewall perimeter. Make sure you're aware of the types of attachments allowed to pass through your email system. For example, any type of executable file is a threat and should be stripped from a message before it's delivered.

Another point of entry may be home devices connecting to your network. Unless you implement a remote access solution that checks for the presence of an operational and up to date antivirus package, you are opening a gaping hole in your security perimeter. New technologies, such as **SSL VPN**, provide the means to check for **personal firewalls** and antivirus applications before allowing a device access to internal resources.

But no matter how up to date you keep your antivirus solution, there is always a delay between the time new malicious code is identified and when your software vendor provides an update.

> ### Key Terms
>
> ***SSL VPN** – A VPN, or Virtual Private Network, is a secure connection between two points, usually at distant locations across the Internet. A VPN connection is often more secure than one with a device on the same internal network. The common method of implementing VPN is with IPSec (Internet Protocol Security). However, a new VPN technology is emerging based on SSL (Secure Sockets Layer). SSL uses certificates and public and private key encryption technology. SSL VPN brings more functionality to the network administrator and is usually much easier to implement than a traditional IPSec VPN implementation.*
>
> ***Personal Firewall** – A personal firewall is an application that resides on and protects an end-user device from external threat agents. It operates in much the same way as a network class firewall.*

Patch management

Unless a system is properly **patched**, an attacker can take advantage of one or more of the many publicly known vulnerabilities. Organizations that delay the implementation of an effective patch management process may face increasing costs associated with attacks that exploit these weaknesses.

Patch management, as referenced in our model, is a set of policies, processes, and tools used to ensure that all systems are at the proper patch level. Processes include:

1. Checking vendor resources for new patches
2. Checking systems for current patch level
3. Regularly testing and applying patches to operating systems, **firmware**, and business applications

These processes can be very time consuming and expensive if done manually. Many larger organizations are prime candidates for one of the many automated patch management solutions available today. Patch management is covered in further detail in Chapter 7.

> **Key Terms**
>
> **Patch** – *A patch is a small fix to a program that corrects a problem. Security patches are regularly released by software and hardware vendors to eliminate newly discovered vulnerabilities in their products.*
>
> **Firmware** – *Put simply, firmware is a program on an integrated circuit or "chip." Many hardware devices contain firmware that performs tasks ranging from boot up activities to fundamental operating and housekeeping tasks.*

Device configuration

Device configuration vulnerabilities are prime targets for malicious attacks. There are two primary paths to secure device configurations. First, we must continue to apply pressure on software vendors to distribute applications in "secure mode." In other words, when I install an application it should install in a secure state. All **services** and add-ons that allow potential network or malicious code access to my system should be disabled by default.

The second path relies on the secure deployment of systems that may not yet support a secure state installation. This is known as "system hardening." System hardening includes:

1. Keeping business applications and operating systems at the most current version – This provides not only the ability to take advantage of new security features but it also ensures the availability of security patches.

2. Ensuring that all systems require appropriate authentication

3. Ensuring that remote access for the purpose of administration or support is controlled by strong authentication methods

4. Disabling any service or port that isn't required for the intended function of the system

5. Controlling device configurations through the use of standard system images that are locked to prevent modification

6. Using the security features included in the operating system to restrict access to information
7. Ensuring systems are properly configured to perform backups

Device configuration is one of the layers over which you have a great deal of control. Make sure you take advantage of it. A detailed look at configuration management is located in Chapter 7.

PUTTING IT ALL TOGETHER

Each of the layers in the JES Model supports the layers below it. Let's take a quick walk up the model to get a better idea of the relationships.

Strong *management support* is necessary to create a business culture in which information security is integrated into each daily task. Guidance on how to apply security is contained in the *security program*. It's through the use of the security program that technical and non-technical employees are given the tools—in the form of policies, standards, guidelines, and procedures—necessary to protect information throughout the enterprise. Employees are trained on and continuously reminded of their roles and responsibilities in the protection of information assets through a strong *user awareness* program. These first three layers form the administrative foundation of a secure environment.

Physical access controls prevent intruders from performing unauthorized tasks, as defined by policies, standards, and guidelines in the security program, that require actual physical contact with a system. These tasks may include the theft or destruction of one or more components of a system, laptop, PDA, etc. *Firewalls* are placed at entry points in the network perimeter as well as into subnets containing sensitive data. They allow only the traffic defined in the policies and standards of the security program to pass. Together, physical access controls and firewalls work to prevent unauthorized access to critical areas of the network. But if an intruder cracks a network firewall, he still has no direct access to information resources.

Logical access controls begin their work once the firewalls and physical controls allow general access. In order to directly access information resources on servers and workstations, an intruder must authenticate to the target system. Authentication may include entering a user ID and password, using a biometric device, a token, or a combination these access control techniques. *IPS/IDS* devices or software help detect and prevent the activities of threat agents that have gained unauthorized access to the network or to a specific resource. They can also help prevent the installation of malware onto servers and end-user devices. Finally, IPS/IDS solutions can detect and react to attempts to circumvent logical access controls by, for example, dictionary or brute force attacks. *Anti-virus (AV) software* supports the IPS/IDS layer by detecting trojans, viruses, worms, and non-viral intrusions such as spyware that may have circumvented its controls. AV and IPS/IDS software protect against attempts by intruders to gain access to information or resources that either assist in cracking logical access controls or in bypassing them altogether. All the layers up to this point are designed to prevent threat agents from reaching an information resource or detecting and removing a threat agent from the network.

Patch management and *device configuration* form the last line of defense against threats. It's the hardening of systems, through the timely application of patches and the careful configuration of system components, that removes the most fundamental security vulnerabilities. Most of the layers below these two serve to protect systems from delayed patch release or implementation as well as weak or nonexistent system security standards and guidelines for secure system configuration.

CHAPTER SUMMARY

The JES model is just one way of looking at defense in depth. It allows us to visualize the various methods required to fully protect critical or sensitive information assets.

The controls included in the model begin with administrative support and preparation, followed by general access controls. The upper layers help to defend assets from intruders who make it past the controls implemented in the first five layers. Finally, the last two layers form the fundamental last line of defense through due diligence in patching and configuring system components.

This chapter is a summary of how each layer works and interfaces with the other layers. The rest of this book explores these concepts in more detail.

CHAPTER 5
MANAGEMENT SUPPORT, DEVELOPING A SECURITY PROGRAM, AND USER AWARENESS

Now that you have a general understanding of the JES layered security model, we begin taking a more detailed look at each layer. In this chapter, we explore what I believe are the three foundational layers of the model: support of management, a well defined and managed security program, and effective user awareness activities.

In this chapter, you'll:

1. Learn the importance of *management support* and some ways to obtain and grow that support

2. Learn the purpose of a *security program*, the components of an effective program, and how to develop and manage those components

3. Learn what role *user awareness* plays in securing your information assets, and how to provide the tools your users need to become security conscious

MANAGEMENT SUPPORT

The first step toward a secure environment is obtaining the support of all levels of management. Support must start with executive management and be pushed down. But getting this support isn't always easy. Here are some of the possible challenges:

1. Security is perceived as a hindrance to efficient business operations.

2. Implementation of security controls, and the resources required to manage those controls, is seen as providing no ROI.

3. The lack of verifiable security incidents leads to management perception that there's little or no risk to information assets.

4. In some cases, information may not be considered a business asset to be protected.

Failure to overcome these challenges can mean a small or nonexistent security budget as well as a general lack of interest in security at all levels of the organization. These two issues combine to present a soft target for all types of attacks. So how do you get management to see the importance of protecting information?

The best way I've found to get management's attention is to build a strong business case that shows the value of security controls—a business case that provides a ROI. I see this as a two-step process.

You can't build a business case unless you understand the business. So the first step is to get involved. Develop a solid understanding of each segment of your organization. This will assist you in determining the importance of various types of information, and how protecting that information contributes to overall cost reductions.

The second step is to establish your credibility by being an enabler rather than a disabler. Managers pushing security often find it difficult to understand the balance between securing information and enhancing operational efficiency. They come to meetings foretelling destruction-of-life-as-we-know-it if information is not completely inaccessible. This may scare away possible supporters as they realize that the proposed information security environment is unrealistic. Always look for the middle path between effective security and operational efficiency. Work with management to identify how various security controls impact employee productivity. Show how security enables the organization to continue operating in the face of internal and external threats. Demonstrate the value of security in ensuring the availability of accurate, timely information.

When you're ready to make your case, present your proposals for security controls from a business perspective; speak the language of executive management. If you're in the healthcare industry, remember to relate your controls to regulatory compliance with HIPAA. If your company is publicly traded, Sarbanes-Oxley is a good place to start in making your point. Whatever industry you're in, or whether you're privately owned or publicly traded, always present your security proposal in terms relevant to the business environment in which your organization operates.

If you still have problems getting what you need, try convincing management to commit resources to perform a risk assessment on one or two of your critical systems. Present these assessments to management, detailing the threats the organization faces and the system vulnerabilities to those threats. Once again, make it real for your audience by defining risk in terms of lost business, loss in shareholder confidence, etc.

Once you obtain management support, you can't assume you'll continue to receive it. It's important to develop metrics to demonstrate the effectiveness of your security program. Examples of successes you can report include:

1. Blocked intrusions reported by your IPS controls
2. Reduction in the number of malware incidents, or the elimination of lost productivity due to such incidents
3. Periodically reworking critical system risk assessments to demonstrate reduced risk levels

In addition to successes, ensure you stay involved in every project to show how security is an integral part of implementation. Remind management that the costs of including security in new system planning is far less than attempting to apply controls once the system is deployed.

Gaining management support is a big step, but it's only the beginning.

Security Program

Once you have management support, you're ready for the second step toward information security—the development of a security program. A security program consists of policies, procedures, guidelines, and baselines. Together, they ensure the following:

1. Definition of administrative, physical, and technical controls
2. Consistent adherence to organizational security requirements
3. Day-to-day management of security activities
4. Defining reasonable and appropriate security for each business critical system

To support these objectives, an effective security program also includes risk assessment activities to test the effectiveness of controls. These activities include penetration testing, vulnerability testing, and policy/procedure gap analysis. In penetration testing, either members of your team or a third party attempts to crack your perimeter controls. Vulnerability testing checks your systems to see if they're open to exploitation by common threats. A policy/procedure gap analysis assesses your current policies and procedures to ensure all relevant areas of security are included in your security program. Finally, a good security program includes an incident response process. Building an effective incident management program is covered in Chapter 9.

Types of security programs

There are two types of security programs—enterprise and system/issue specific. An enterprise security program contains the policies, standards, and guidelines that provide the general security canopy under which all systems operate. They're supported by general baselines and procedures that apply to all facets of the information environment.

System or issue specific security programs target individual critical systems or organizational issues. Organizational issues might include:

1. How to define and implement business continuity
2. Use of a specific methodology for change management, development, etc.
3. Framework within which cutting-edge technology may be used, including email, handheld devices, wireless networking, portable storage devices, etc.
4. Regulatory compliance
5. Tools and methods for managing risk
6. Physical security
7. Administrative security

The components of a system or issue specific program augment the enterprise program by targeting concerns that are unique to certain operational areas of the business.

Resource requirements

As you might expect, the greatest direct cost associated with the development and management of a security program is personnel. Some organizations outsource the complete security effort. This may be a good option if you just don't want to be bothered with the mechanics of data protection. However, you're still responsible for how the outsource vendor performs, the policies put in place, and the effectiveness of the services provided. This approach always makes me a little nervous. I like to have more control over my security environment. It can also be more expensive than doing it yourself if you're not careful. The biggest benefit of this approach is that you have a professional security team monitoring your network and managing incident response.

Another approach is to do it all yourself. This is not a bad way to implement security, assuming you or a member of your team has the skills, time, and desire to build and manage a security program. For a small organization, this could also mean a long term commitment by most or all of your IS department. Unless you're working for a large company with a dedicated security staff, this may not be the best use of your human resources.

A third way to implement a security program is to engage security consultants to work with your team to develop appropriate policies, procedures, guidelines, and baselines. As your team works through the development and implementation processes, ensure that a knowledge transfer takes place. This provides you with a professionally built program, a trained staff, and you don't have to commit your entire IS team to the project. Once the program is in place, you can outsource the parts of it you decide are more efficiently managed by dedicated service organizations. I prefer this approach. It optimizes your in-house staff while providing an adequate level of security to the organization.

In addition to personnel costs, there are technical costs related to monitoring and measuring the effectiveness of the program. Without the right tools and processes in place, you can't continuously improve your ability to protect your information assets while managing overall costs. Some of the tools you may need include:

1. A port scanner to check for server and workstation vulnerabilities
2. A network scanner to identify network vulnerabilities
3. Penetration testing equipment and software
4. Network monitors
5. An intrusion prevention system

Finally, you will need resources to disseminate information to your staff. As we'll discuss later in this chapter, employee awareness activities and employee training are key to securing your information assets.

Building policies

Policies form the basic framework of a security program. At the program level, policies represent senior management's security objectives. At the system level, they provide rules for the construction and operation of specific systems. Whether program or system specific, policies help prevent inconsistencies by forming the basis for detailed standards, guidelines, and procedures. They also serve as tools to inform employees about appropriate activities and restrictions required for regulatory compliance. Finally, policies make clear management's expectations of employee involvement in protecting information assets.

When building a policy, make sure it's clear and flexible. It shouldn't provide so much detail that it forces unreasonable constraints on operational areas of your business. Leave room to make management decisions that fit particular challenges as they arise.

Program policies establish the security program. They provide its form and character. The sections that make up a program policy include purpose, scope, responsibilities, and compliance.

Purpose includes the objectives of the program, such as:

1. Improved recovery times
2. Reduced costs or downtime due to loss of data
3. Reduction in errors for both system changes and operational activities
4. Regulatory compliance
5. Management of overall confidentiality, integrity, and availability

Scope provides guidance on whom and what are covered by the policy. Coverage may include:

1. Facilities
2. Lines of business
3. Employees or departments
4. Technology
5. Processes

Responsibilities for the implementation and management of the policy are assigned in this section. Organizational units or individuals are potential assignment candidates.

Compliance provides for the policy's enforcement. Describe oversight activities and disciplinary considerations clearly. But the contents of this section are meaningless unless an effective awareness program is in place.

System specific policies provide the framework for system and issue specific security programs. Like program policies, system policies should be flexible enough to allow managers to make effective operational decisions while safeguarding the confidentiality, integrity, and availability of information assets. System policies typically address two areas—security objectives and operational security standards.

Policies that describe security objectives clearly define measurable, achievable goals. These goals focus on data owner directives intended to protect specific systems. The policies are written to take into account the system's functional requirements as seen by business users. Because policies apply constraints on how a system or a technology may be deployed and used, there's always a danger that meeting security objectives may adversely impact operational efficiency. It's important to balance reduction in risk with the cost associated with potential losses in productivity.

Operational security standards provide a clear set of rules for operating and managing a system or a technology. As with system policy objectives, these rules shouldn't be so restrictive that they paralyze your organization. In addition, the administrative burden associated with managing and enforcing overly restrictive policies may cost your organization more than the business impact you're trying to protect against. The elements of a system/issue specific policy include purpose, objectives, scope, roles and responsibilities, compliance, and policy owner and contact information.

Purpose defines the challenge management is addressing. Challenges might include regulatory constraints, protection of highly sensitive data, or the safe use of certain technologies. In some cases, it may be necessary to define terms. It's important that everyone affected by the policy clearly understands its content. Finally, clearly state the conditions under which the policy is applicable.

Objectives may include actions and configurations prohibited or controlled. Although they're normally defined outside a policy, circumstances and organizational practices may require placing certain standards and guidelines in this section. In any case, it's in this section that you define the results you expect from policy enforcement.

Scope specifies where, when, how, and to whom the policy applies.

Roles and Responsibilities identify the business units or individuals responsible for the various areas of implementation and enforcement of the policy.

Compliance is just as important in a system or issue level policy as it is in a program policy. You should clearly state the possible consequences of not conforming to the standards and guidelines listed in Objectives.

Policy Owner and Contact Information lists the person who is ultimately responsible for managing the policy. Since the data owner is responsible for defining the protection required for a specific system, she may be a good choice for policy owner. Ensure that contact information for the policy owner is kept up to date. This allows individuals responsible for implementing systems under the policy to contact the policy owner for clarification on standards and guidelines.

The final step in the construction of a policy is approval by senior management. Without their approval and support, a policy isn't worth very much. One way to ensure management support is to involve relevant areas of the business in the construction of each policy. This helps prevent the perception that information security policies, and information security in general, are an IS problem. It also nurtures a feeling of ownership across the organization. Managers are more willing to support operational restrictions that result in clear business value they helped to define.

Although you can start with a blank sheet, I recommend you look at some example policies before committing to writing everything yourself. A good place to start is the SANS Security Policy Project page at http://www.sans.org/resources/policies/.

Policy implementation

After gaining management support and sign off, implementation planning begins. The roll out of a new policy should include the following activities:

1. Ensure that everyone is aware of the new policy. Post it on your Intranet, send a notification email, or perform whatever other mass distribution actions work well within your organization.

2. Discuss the contents of the policy at management and staff meetings. It's important during these discussions to include a review of the intended results of following the policy. This helps your organization's employees see the standards and guidelines from the proper perspective.

3. Conduct training sessions. Training should occur at three levels—management, general staff, and technical staff.

a. Management training is intended to educate managers about their role in enforcement and compliance activities. It should include a "big picture" view of where the policy fits in the overall security program.

b. General staff training is provided to all staff levels in the organization. In addition to making employees aware of the contents of the policy, it should also address any questions about how the objectives, standards, and guidelines will impact day-to-day operation of the business. Staff training should always precede any attempts to sanction an employee for failure to follow a security policy.

c. Technical staff training is typically provided for the IS staff. The focus of this training is how the new policy affects existing system or network configurations and baselines.

4. Develop supporting standards, guidelines, procedures, and baselines.
5. Implement a user awareness program.

Standards, guidelines, procedures, and baselines

These four security program elements have shown up in almost every topic covered so far in this book. They are the means whereby engineers, programmers, managers, and users adhere to security policy. The relationships between these areas of compliance activity are depicted in Figure 5-1.

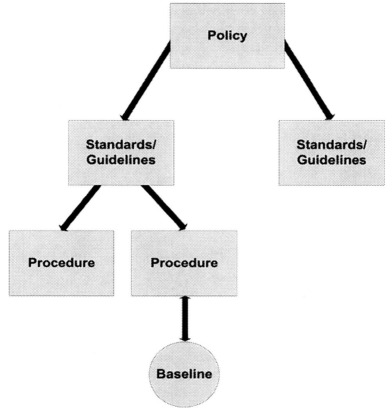

Figure 5 - 1: Policies, Standards/Guidelines, Procedures, and Baselines

Policies provide general statements of security goals and objectives approved by management. From those policies, technical and administrative teams define standards and guidelines to support the policies. Standards specify mandatory or prohibited hardware and software configurations, and compulsory processes for implementation, operation, and use of all or specific information systems. The scope of a standard typically depends on whether it's supporting a program policy or a system/issue specific policy.

Too many standards can place onerous restrictions on operational managers and staff. On the other hand, there must be consistency in the application of security policies. This is where guidelines add value. Guidelines provide recommended actions, hardware and software configurations, and processes in line with governing policies. Although managers must consider guidelines in day-to-day activities, they have some latitude in deciding how to implement them. The best practice principle of implementing security that is reasonable and appropriate is a good approach to enforcing guidelines. Each operation within your organization should be considered a unique opportunity to interpret guidelines in a way that protects your information assets while maintaining operational efficiency.

Once your standards and guidelines are defined, procedures should be developed to implement them. Procedures are detailed, step by step approaches to performing a task. Examples include:

1. Building a file and print server
2. Building a local area network
3. Deploying email capability to a user workstation
4. Configuring a smart phone
5. Processing accounts payable

Well defined, documented, and operationally integrated procedures ensure consistency in policy compliance.

Finally, baselines are the minimum level of security allowable in the configuration of hardware and software. For example, when building a server, the baseline configuration must be applied to provide the level of security absolutely required by policy, standards, etc. Additional security may be added, as long as it doesn't reduce the level of protection below that provided by the baseline configuration.

Policies, standards, guidelines, procedures, and baselines provide the framework for program and system/issue specific security programs. It's upon this framework that all decisions concerning the remaining layers in the JES model are based.

USER AWARENESS

User awareness completes the administrative foundation of a secure information processing environment. It is through an effective awareness program that a desire to meet policy objectives becomes part of your organization's culture.

Building an Awareness Program

The first step in building an awareness program is to understand the differences in the way each area of the business perceives your policies and objectives. One of the easiest ways to accomplish this is the creation of a cross-functional awareness team. The assimilation of different perspectives provides insights into the best way to design awareness materials.

An awareness message should be short and to the point. The content of the message, whether delivered electronically or by some hard copy method, should address personal as well as organizational concerns. This makes the message more meaningful to individual users. An example of this approach, the "Did you know..." format, is depicted in Figure 5-2.

In this example, the message includes information relevant to the users' use of the Internet in general. It warns them of the possible problems associated with not practicing care when responding to messages. It also uses a short reference to the existence of a company policy related to this issue. By making users aware of personal as well as business risk, there's a better chance they'll remember the awareness message you're delivering.

There are other ways to deliver awareness messages. Table tent cards in the company lunch room, voice mail announcements, and posters are just a few. Be creative. Continuous use of the same old delivery methods might result in employee disinterest.

The creation of unique delivery methods may not always be necessary. Review the general training and awareness programs that exist in your organization today. These might include the following:

1. New employee training
2. Infrastructure training for new network engineers
3. Application training for specific system users
4. Operational training for system managers

> **Did You Know ...**
> ...**criminals** often create **Spoof Sites** that look like legitimate sites to **Trick You** into giving them your information?
>
> Often these attacks send users an **email request to update**

> **their credit card information** by following the attached link. The link takes you to a site that often looks like the real site but **is a hoax to steal your identity.**
>
> It is **against our company's policy** to use workstations from any location for any activities that are not related to the business of the company.
>
> **How to protect yourself:**
> **Never click on a link** within an email **asking you to update personal information** such as credit card numbers or passwords. Go directly to the appropriate business site, and navigate to account management sections.

Figure 5 - 2: Sample Awareness Message

Building awareness training into each of these processes is an effective way to build user awareness with tools and content appropriate for various audiences.

Measuring results

User awareness is a continuous process. Like all processes, it's always valuable to understand the effectiveness of your approach. Clear measures of effectiveness help you adjust your awareness program to meet management security objectives. Some ways to gauge user awareness include on-line tests on your intranet, formal surveys, and informal staff meetings to discuss security issues.

Regardless of the method appropriate for your organization, don't skip this step. Make sure you're getting value for your awareness program dollars.

CHAPTER SUMMARY

The three foundational elements of a secure information processing environment are management support, an effective security program, and continuous user awareness activities.

Management support is gained through a thorough understanding of business challenges associated with information confidentiality, integrity, and availability. Presentations to management for budget and project approval must approach security from the perspective of how business value will be enhanced. Reports containing metrics showing the effectiveness of security program activities help to ensure continued support.

Security policies clearly define the challenges addressed, security objectives, roles and responsibilities, and compliance considerations. Roll out new policies with appropriate training.

User awareness is a fundamental requirement for information security effectiveness. Consistently meeting security objectives requires a shift in user thinking—a shift in an organization's culture. Be creative in your approach, and keep the message simple. Use metrics to determine the effectiveness of your message delivery methods.

CHAPTER 6
ACCESS CONTROLS

Once the security program is in place, it's time to start building the security infrastructure. In this chapter, we'll look at what it takes to control access to your information assets. You'll:

1. Learn how to structure your security program to provide *administrative* controls
2. Learn the various components of *physical* and *logical* access controls
3. Review the challenges associated with implementing *biometrics*
4. Learn about the various ways to control access to your network when using *wireless* LAN technology
5. Explore the different types of *firewalls* and how to deploy them to protect your perimeter and segments of your internal network

WHAT ARE ACCESS CONTROLS?

It isn't enough to build a world-class data center; you actually have to grant your employees access to it. But how do you control access in a way that enables the delivery of information when and where your users need it while preventing unauthorized persons from gaining access? Further, how do you protect the integrity of your data from the intentional and unintentional actions of both groups? The answer to these questions is the effective implementation of administrative, physical, and logical (technical) access controls.

Access controls manage physical and logical access to system and network resources through policies, procedures, access control software, access control devices, and physical barriers. Their application should be based on a careful balance between mitigating risk to the business and maintaining operational efficiency. Locking down your information assets so tightly that it's difficult for your users to access what they need in order to do their jobs might result in a greater negative impact on your business, over time, than potential threats.

The controls included in each of the three main categories—administrative, physical, and logical—can be further classified as preventive, detective, and corrective. In this chapter, we'll focus on the preventive and detective aspects of access controls. We'll cover corrective controls in Chapter 9. Preventive controls act as deterrents or barriers to unauthorized access. Detective controls support preventive efforts by monitoring for activities or conditions caused by the failure of deterrents or barriers.

ADMINISTRATIVE CONTROLS

There isn't a separate layer in the security model labeled Administrative Controls. This is because administrative controls consist of the policies, procedures, standards, and baselines that make up an organization's Security Program. Security Programs were covered in Chapter 5. In this chapter, we'll take a closer look at specific access control policies and procedures that should be part of every program.

Access Controls

Preventive

Preventive administrative controls consist primarily of management policies and procedures designed to protect against unwanted employee behavior. These controls include:

1. Separation of duties
2. Business continuity and DR planning/testing
3. Proper hiring practices
4. Proper processing of terminations

Separation of duties

Most positive business outcomes are the result of properly executed processes. When a single individual performs all steps in a process, that person has the opportunity to perform an intentional or unintentional act that may compromise the confidentiality, integrity, or availability of your data. Worse, fraud and embezzlement are easier to commit.

To eliminate or mitigate opportunities for unwanted behavior, separate each process into discrete tasks. Divide these tasks between two or more individuals. This creates an environment in which intentional wrongdoing requires **collusion.** There's also a better chance that mistakes will be caught as the process moves from one set of eyes to another.

> ***Key Terms***
>
> ***Collusion*** *– Within the context of information security, collusion is the agreement between two or more individuals to commit an unlawful or unethical act.*

Business continuity and disaster recovery planning/testing

Business continuity activities help protect the availability of your information assets. Included in these activities are incident response and disaster recovery processes designed to prevent security incidents from having a major impact on your business. Business continuity is examined in Chapter 8.

Proper hiring practices

Since the majority of security incidents are caused by the action or inaction of your employees, hiring the right people is a key administrative control. As a manager, there are two activities you can implement as part of your hiring process—background and reference checks.

Background checks might simply consist of a simple phone call to local law enforcement authorities for a records check. If you believe a more comprehensive check is required, there are online services that quickly perform national checks on prospective employees. The detail level of the check, and the magnitude of the security cost you're willing to absorb during the hiring process, should depend on the sensitivity of the information for which the potential employee will be responsible.

It's common practice for managers to conduct reference checks on potential new hires. However, these checks often deal only with the person's ability to perform. This type of check is probably sufficient if the data the person is to process daily has little value to your organization. However, if the person is to regularly process sensitive or business critical information, there are two additional reference checks you will want to consider.

Checking character references is a good way to determine whether a person can be trusted. Does the person consistently make commitments on which he follows through? Present and former employers may not be the best sources for this information. Lawsuits due to character-based comments made by managers about former employees have resulted in a large number of organizational policies against providing this kind of information. So you should include a request for non-employer references as part of the employment application process.

Credit checks are another way to determine if a person is right for an open position. A credit check is not necessarily performed to determine if someone is susceptible to bribery—although this is important information if your organization possesses one or more trade secrets that are critical to your competitive advantage. Another important reason to perform a credit check is to determine the maturity of the individual and her willingness to accept responsibility. You can tell quite a bit from a credit report in which it's obvious that a person is consistently late attending to financial obligations, or doesn't attend to them at all.

Proper processing of terminations

During a person's employment with your organization, you might give him access to various information resources. In addition, you might issue him keys, badges, etc. When he leaves, the person processing his termination should follow a well-documented process for removing his logical and physical access to all business assets, including your data.

It isn't always easy to remove all data access rights from an employee who is leaving. Disabling or deleting operating system accounts is the easy part. It's finding all application and remote access accounts that may bypass operating system security that presents the greatest challenge. If your organization is small, I recommend maintaining a spreadsheet with a row listing each employee. In addition to the employee's name, also include columns for each application and corresponding user ID to which the employee has access. Remember that the content of this spreadsheet is sensitive data. As a minimal safeguard, you should password-protect the spreadsheet file. A better solution is to purchase an inexpensive encryption program to encrypt the file.

Larger companies may want to consider an Identity and Account Management solution. As the number of accounts increases, the cost of tracking and managing the location of accounts increases. The typical result of a manual solution is a long list of **stale accounts** in various applications. In addition to each of these accounts becoming a potential "gotcha" during an audit, they pose a significant risk to your organization. They contain passwords that never change. They also provide former employees with the means to access your information assets.

> ### *Key Terms*
>
> ***Stale Accounts*** *– An account, either for system or network access, which has not been used during a predetermined period. For example, some organizations may consider an account stale if it hasn't been used for 60 days. The period used depends on the work, vacation, and travel habits of an organization's employees. In any case, stale accounts present significant security vulnerabilities. They should be disabled or deleted.*

Finally, ensure employees terminated for cause are not left alone within the physical limits of your organization after you inform them of their employment status. An employee terminated for cause should be escorted to his desk, watched as he packs his personal belongings, and escorted off the premises. Remove access to the network during the termination meeting. Most employers for whom I've worked provided notice to Security ahead of the termination discussion. Relevant accounts were disabled before the terminated employee left his manager's office. Finally, inform the security officers responsible for your facility to deny future access to the terminated individual.

Detective

Detective administrative controls are used to determine how well the security program is working. The most common controls in this category are:

1. Security reviews and audits
2. Mandatory vacations
3. Background investigations of current employees
4. Rotation of duties

Security reviews and audits

Reviews and audits are an important part of any security program. Not only should you develop a process to periodically check system, network, and procedure compliance, but you should also consider an annual third party assessment.

There are four areas of compliance you should include in an assessment: program policies and processes, system policies and processes, vulnerability tests, and penetration tests. It isn't always possible to look at all four areas each year. Internal resource or cost constraints may make this difficult or impossible. In such cases, I recommend separating the four compliance areas into a rotating annual schedule. For example, a three-year review and audit cycle might look like Figure 6-1.

The first year's activities include a policy and procedure gap analysis. The assessing organization provides a final report listing areas where, in their opinion, improvements in policies and procedures can be made to improve the security program. It's important to remember that the risk management principles described in Chapter 3 should be applied to any assessment recommendation.

Access Controls

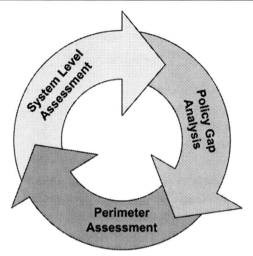

Figure 6 - 1: Example Review/Audit Cycle

During the second year's assessment, the assessing organization tests for vulnerabilities in the network perimeter. This assessment includes perimeter penetration tests and the use of tools and techniques to determine if well-known vulnerabilities exist in your perimeter device configurations.

The activities in the third year are similar to those in year two; the primary difference is scope. In year three, the focus is on some or all of an organization's business systems. The cycle begins again in year four.

You might also have to undergo regulatory audits by independent auditors. Regulatory compliance with legislation like the HIPAA and Sarbanes-Oxley should be an important part of your internal reviews and audits.

How you approach review and audit is up to you. Just ensure it's an active part of your security program.

Mandatory vacations

This is a control that's usually viewed with raised eyebrows. I know I initially questioned the effectiveness of making employees take time off. However, mandatory vacations can add significant value to your detection efforts.

When an employee takes a week off, someone else typically has to take over her responsibilities. This new set of eyes can identify intentional and unintentional actions taken by the absent employee, which may negatively affect the confidentiality, integrity, or availability of your information assets. Mandatory vacations can also act as a deterrent to possible intentional malicious or self-serving activities. If a person knows he has to take a vacation, he might be less likely to perform illegal or unethical acts.

Another reason your employees should take time off is to reduce personal stress levels. An employee who is under a lot of stress each day, and refuses to take time off, is more likely to make a mistake that compromises the integrity of your information.

Background investigations of existing employees

It might not be enough to conduct background checks during the hiring process. Employees who are promoted to positions in which they handle more sensitive data are candidates for an additional background check. It's also a good idea to conduct periodic checks on employees who consistently handle highly sensitive or critical information. In both cases, investigations can reveal activities that constitute possible security policy violations or the potential for the commission of such violations.

Rotation of duties

The benefits of rotation of duties are almost the same as those realized from mandatory vacations. Employees are less likely to commit a voluntary illegal or unethical act when they know another set of eyes will regularly view the results of their work. A side benefit is the potential to cross-train multiple employees to perform important business tasks.

The administrative controls we've reviewed are only as effective as your employees' level of understanding of the policies, procedures, standards, and guidelines. This understanding must be combined with the willingness on the part of supervisors and managers to adhere to and enforce your security program. Both employee and manager compliance is dependant upon strong security awareness. Unless employees are aware of your security expectations, they can't be expected to comply with them. And unless your employees are convinced of the need for the extra effort required every day to secure your information assets, enforcement will require constant effort and may result in employee resentment and intentional non-compliance.

PHYSICAL CONTROLS

Administrative controls rely on the willing compliance of managers and employees. Physical controls rely on the proper application of physical barriers and deterrents to control behavior. It's through the use of physical controls that an organization controls physical access to facilities and systems. They also assist in maintaining the operating environments necessary to continue information processing and delivery activities.

Before we move into the specifics of various physical controls, it's important to understand their proper application and purpose. Figure 6-2 is a graphic example of one way to view the layers of a physical security solution.

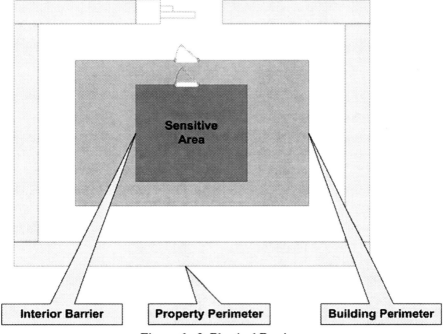

Figure 6 - 2: Physical Barriers

Physical security controls are meant to detect and delay the passage of an intruder as she moves inward toward sensitive areas within your facility. Following the principle of diversity in design, the use of different controls at each entry point help to attain this objective.

Preventive

Preventive physical controls provide an environment in which to safely process information as well as barriers to unauthorized access to systems. These controls include:

1. Alternate power sources
2. Flood management
3. Backups
4. Fences
5. Security guards
6. Locks
7. Biometrics
8. Location
9. Fire suppression systems

Alternate power sources

Under normal circumstances, it's reasonable to rely on the power company as a clean, stable source of power. But as we've all experienced, there are no guarantees that the power coming into your building will always be available. Alternate power sources are used to provide power when utility power fails.

In this section, we'll discuss two types of power sources: uninterruptible power supplies (UPS) and generators. A UPS is a battery-powered device that provides power for a short period. It is typically used to provide power long enough to properly shut down your servers (preventing data or system damage) or to switch to a generator. You shouldn't rely on your UPS to indefinitely continue normal operations.

If you must keep one or more servers up during a long-term power outage, you should consider a generator. With a continuous supply of fuel, a generator can indefinitely supply power to your data center. Because switching to generator power can take a few minutes, it's necessary to supplement your generator with a UPS to prevent a hard shutdown of your data center equipment; the UPS provides power for the time it takes to bring your generator online.

Access Controls

Flood management

The first preventive measure in preventing water in your facility is locating it in a geographic area that doesn't regularly flood. Next, you should place water sensors in your data center. If you have raised floors, place them under the floor. If not, place them in areas most likely to experience flooding first. Detecting the presence of water in your data center might not allow you to do anything to continue operating, but it can provide enough warning so you can protect your equipment from damage. This process can consist of removing equipment from the affected area or simply shutting down equipment that's impractical to move. In either case, damage is minimized, allowing your business to quickly return to normal operation.

You should also consider mounting your servers at least two to three inches above the floor. Purchasing racks in which to place your servers should make this a simple task.

Backups

For the past fifteen years, I've taught the engineers working for me that the most important task they perform each day is ensuring the proper backup of critical business data. Backing up your systems is the single most important activity you perform if you want to have any chance at all of recovering from a system, data center, or facility failure.

In this section, we'll discuss three types of backups: full, incremental, and differential. A full backup copies all files from your production storage devices (normally disk) to your backup media. Although tape has been the backup media of choice for many years, backup to disk is becoming popular. A full backup provides for the fastest restore time. If you have to rebuild a server in your data center or at a disaster recovery location, you only have to restore a single backup. However, many organizations can't perform full backups every night.

Full backups take a long time to run. If your data center is running production jobs twenty-four hours a day, you only have a small processing window in which to run your nightly backups. Incremental and differential backups can help.

An incremental backup copies to your backup media all files that changed since the last backup. This requires a much smaller backup window. But it takes much longer to restore if you have to rebuild a system. Figure 6-3 depicts a common incremental backup schedule.

Just Enough Security

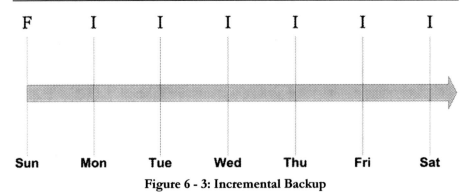

Figure 6 - 3: Incremental Backup

In this example, a full backup is performed each Sunday night when there are no production jobs running. An incremental backup is run on each of the other nights of the week. This is a great solution for minimizing production downtime to perform backups. But what happens if the system backed up in this way fails?

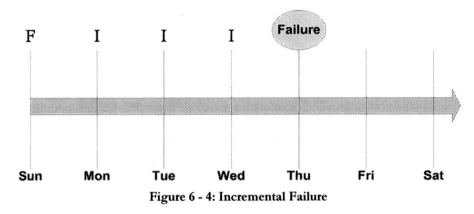

Figure 6 - 4: Incremental Failure

In Figure 6-4, the system backed up in our example fails on Thursday, prior to the Thursday night backup. Since the backups on Monday, Tuesday, and Wednesday contain only the files that changed since the previous night's backup, the data center staff must restore the full backup from Sunday, followed by each of the incremental backups in the correct sequence. The restore process is depicted in Figure 6-5. This can be a lengthy process.

Access Controls

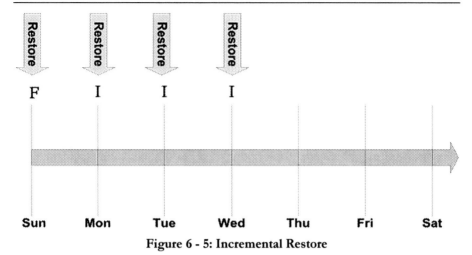

Figure 6 - 5: Incremental Restore

Differential backups provide a backup and restore solution that combines a measure of the reduced backup time of incremental backups with a portion of the reduced restore time inherent in a full backup method. A differential backup copies to your backup media files that have changed since your last full backup.

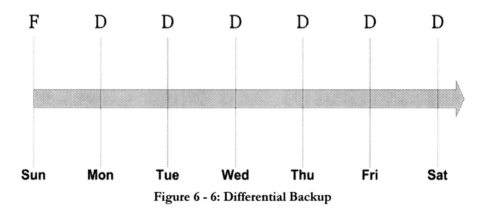

Figure 6 - 6: Differential Backup

Figure 6-6 represents a typical differential backup schedule. It looks the same as the incremental approach in Figure 6-3. However, there is one important difference. Since the differential backups copy all files that have changed since the last full backup, the backup time increases as each day passes; more files are changed as the week progresses.

Figure 6-7 depicts a differential restore with a system failure on Thursday, prior to the Thursday backup. Instead of a full restore and three partial restores, a differential restore consists of a full restore and the restoration of the last differential backup.

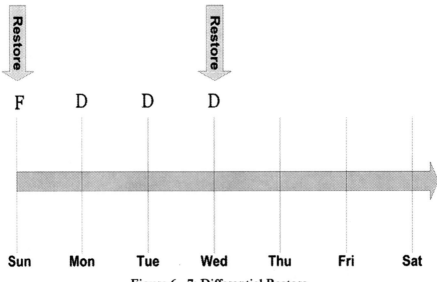

Figure 6 - 7: Differential Restore

Once you create your backups, you need to keep them in a safe place. A fireproof safe in your data center might seem like a good idea. But what happens if your data center is destroyed or is inaccessible? How do you get to your tapes? At least one set of recovery tapes should be kept at an off-site location. For example, if you perform incremental backups, the last full backup and all subsequent incremental backups should be kept in a secure off-site facility. Even if your primary backup method is to disk, you should have a full recovery set of data at another location.

The final consideration in backup planning is the protection of the information stored on tapes. Tapes can be stolen or lost. Sensitive information, like health information protected under the HIPAA, can be compromised. You should consider encrypting sensitive information as it's copied to tape. Most, if not all, backup software supports this feature.

Fences

Fences are a physical barrier used primarily to deter casual trespassers. Most organizations are not prepared to install eight foot fencing topped with razor wire. Unless you are working on products

Access Controls

essential to national security, this kind of barrier can present an overwhelming image to potential customers—not to mention the cost.

To a casual intruder, a fence of any kind communicates the presence of a no-trespass zone. On the other hand, fencing by itself is not very effective against a determined intruder. But coupled with other controls, it can be a component of a very effective physical security plan. Controls that can be used to supplement fencing include continuous lighting, closed circuit cameras, physical intrusion detection devices, and guards.

Guards

Guards, both roving and stationary, provide a control that can react to the unexpected. With all the technology available today, a human being still adds the most value when intuition and common sense are required. Further, once an intruder decides to penetrate your physical perimeter, guards are the best defense against that intruder actually reaching your assets. The obvious downside to the use of security guards is cost. Costs associated with hiring, salary and benefits, equipment and uniforms, training, etc. must be weighed against the potential business impact of a physical intrusion.

Locks

We'll cover three common types of locking mechanisms in this chapter—badge readers, combination locks, and push-button/cipher locks.

Badge readers are electronic devices that may or may not be connected to a central security system. Central security systems facilitate efficient management of authorized access and the monitoring of entry points.

A card, or badge, is used to release a lock controlled by the reader. Based on the type of reader used, lock release can occur by direct contact with the reader or through **proximity** detection.

Key Terms

Proximity detection *– Some security devices used for physical or logical access control can detect, without physical contact, the presence of an individual authorized to gain entry to a facility or to log in to a workstation. These are called proximity detection devices. A proximity detection solution normally consists of a reader at the point of entry, or at the workstation, and a badge or other device in the possession of the employee. When the reader and the employee are within a predefined distance of each other, the user is authenticated to an access control system.*

Security systems based on badge readers are often easy for users to operate. A simple swipe of a card or simply walking up to a proximity activated reader can facilitate entry. There's no combination to remember or key to locate. A disadvantage of a badge system is cost, including the purchase of the readers and the purchase, issuance, and tracking of the badges. A bigger problem may be that the unreported loss of a badge or token might compromise your physical security efforts.

Two basic types of locks used to secure physical assets when badge systems are not used are key locks and keyless locks. A key lock can be a simple lock affixed to a door (deadlock, handle locks, etc.) or a padlock. Key locks are inexpensive, and your users are familiar with their use. A disadvantage with using key locks is the management of keys. One lost key, and all affected locks must be replaced. There is also the risk that keys will be lost or reproduced without your knowledge—thus elevating the risk of unwanted physical access.

Keyless locks include:

1. Mechanical and electronic rotary combination locks
2. Mechanical Push-button locks
3. Cipher locks

Rotary combination locks are another familiar locking method. Authorized users are provided with a combination used to enter a sensitive area. Mechanical, rotary, combination locks are inexpensive and easily replaced if an employee leaves the company or if you believe the combination has been shared with unauthorized personnel. Although electronic rotary locks are not inexpensive, changing the combination is easily accomplished by a lock administrator.

Push-button locks are mechanical devices with numbered buttons. A person seeking to gain access to a secured area enters a code to release the locking mechanism. Changes to the combination are often made by disassembling the lock.

Cipher locks are roughly the electronic equivalent of a push-button lock. Although more expensive than its mechanical counterpart, the cipher lock can provide significant advantages. Several different access codes can be entered into the lock. Using a lock that supports multiple codes provides the capability to provide each authorized user with a unique code. And you can assign a special lock administrator code for code maintenance.

Many cipher locks also support a panic code. Users approaching the lock under duress simply enter the panic code, and an alarm is initiated. Some cipher lock systems can be connected to a central access control computer. Like many badge systems, this provides for centralized management of access codes, access monitoring, etc.

The obvious disadvantage of combination and push-button/cipher locks is the possibility that a combination or code will be compromised. One method an intruder might use to obtain a combination or code is shoulder-surfing. Another is the use of social engineering.

Although locks are the most common method used to secure physical assets, they should be considered only as a delaying tactic. Locks are quite vulnerable to the efforts of a determined intruder. In addition to the possible compromise of keys, combinations, badges, or codes, a good crowbar may be "good enough" for quick entry into one of your locked areas.

Biometrics

Biometrics is the use of unique human physical characteristics to identify and authenticate authorized personnel. You can use these devices to control doors, gates, etc. Although I'm presenting a detailed discussion of biometrics as they apply to physical access controls, all the principles discussed also apply to network or device identification and authentication.

There are several human physical traits that can be used to uniquely identify a person. They include:

1. The retina, specifically the blood vessel pattern inside the eye
2. Voice patterns
3. Signature dynamics
4. Finger or hand geometry, including fingerprints, finger or hand height and width, etc.
5. The features of the iris, the colored area of the eye surrounding the pupil

Of these, the iris, retina, and finger/hand geometry are the most effective. A person's voice may be recorded and signatures can be forged.

When considering the purchase and implementation of a biometrics identification system, you should address the following eight critical success factors:

1. Accuracy
2. Speed
3. Resistance to counterfeiting
4. Reliability
5. Data storage requirements
6. Enrollment time
7. Perceived intrusiveness
8. User acceptance

Accuracy

Biometric devices have improved significantly over the past several years. However, there are still no guarantees of 100% accuracy. It's your responsibility to select the level of inaccuracy that you and your employees can tolerate. When judging error rates, consider the principle types of errors—Type I and Type II. Type I errors include all instances in which a biometric system denies access to an authorized user. The identification of an unauthorized user as an authorized user is an example of a Type II error. By adjusting the sensitivity of the biometric sensor, you can increase or decrease the occurrence of each error type. However, as you decrease Type I errors, you might increase Type II errors. The opposite is also true.

The key objective in implementing a biometric system is the proper balance between these two error types. The most common method is to focus on the Cross-over Error Rate (CER). This is the point at which the frequency of Type I errors and the frequency of Type II errors are equal. When shopping for the right system for your business, the CER is the best indicator of overall accuracy.

Access Controls

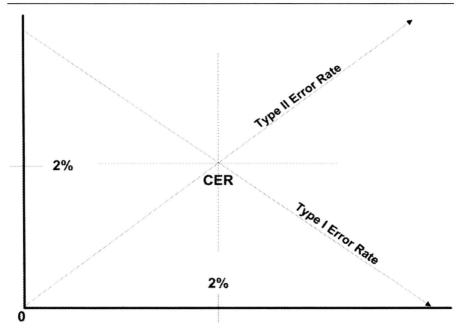

Figure 6 - 8: CER and Error Rate Relationship

CER is expressed as a percentage. Lower values are better. Values of two to five percent are generally considered acceptable.

Speed

When considering the probability that your users will accept the use of biometrics, the speed at which a sensor and its controlling software accept or reject authentication attempts is the most important factor. The effective throughput, or how many users a biometric sensor can process in a given period, is a function of the entire authentication process. Figure 6-9 depicts the several stages involved. Acceptable throughput is typically five seconds per person or six to ten people per minute. User frustration begins to set in at lower throughput rates.

Just Enough Security

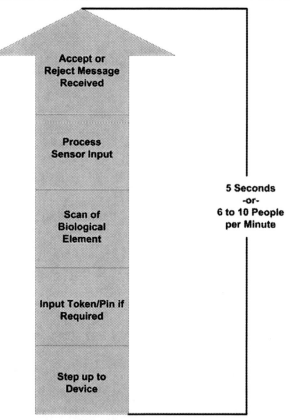

Figure 6 - 9: Biometric Authentication Process

Resistance to counterfeiting

I've already stated that signature dynamics and voice recognition are not necessarily the best choice for biological recognition because of the potential for forgery or the use of recorded voice. But systems that use other body parts might also be susceptible to counterfeiting. For example, some early biometric systems allowed an intruder to use lifted finger or hand prints to gain entry. Today's systems are, in general, more sophisticated; they use the entire geometry of a finger or hand instead of just the line patterns that make up prints. Make sure to ask the right questions if you consider using a biometric access control system. When possible, request a demonstration of the system's resistance to counterfeiting.

Access Controls

Reliability

Sensors must continue to operate at a low CER between failures. A gradual degradation in throughput affects user acceptability and organizational productivity.

Data storage requirements

The amount of storage necessary to support a biometric system depends on what data is actually stored. Voice recognition systems might use a great deal of storage; voice files are usually large. Current finger architecture recognition technology, however, simply stores a relatively small **hash value** created when a user is enrolled. Whenever a sensor scans the finger again, it recomputes the hash value and compares it to the stored value. Whatever biometric solution you choose, make sure you understand the impact on your storage environment.

Key Terms

Hash Value *– A hash value is produced by feeding information to a special computer program. The program converts the input into a fixed length value. The same input should always produce the same hash value. In the case of biometrics, a significant amount of information may be gathered by a finger sensor. This information can be reduced to a much smaller hash value. Another advantage of using hash values instead of raw information is the inability of an attacker to derive from the hash value the original input from which it was created.*

Enrollment time

Another factor influencing user acceptance is the time required to enroll a new user into the biometric system. An acceptable enrollment duration is usually two minutes or less per person. This enrollment rate not only reduces employee frustration but it also helps reduce administrative costs associated with system management.

Perceived intrusiveness

Second only to throughput, the amount of personal intrusiveness a sensor presents to your employees is a major determinant when assessing user acceptance. The following is a list of common fears that grow out of biometric implementations.

1. Fear that the company stores unique personal information
2. Fear that the company is collecting personal health information (retinal scans look at patterns that are also used to determine certain health conditions) for insurance purposes
3. Fear that the red light in retinal scanning sensors is physically harmful
4. Fear of contracting diseases through contact with publicly used sensors

The best way to deal with these issues is to hold open and honest discussions about how the systems work, the health risks involved, and how the organization plans to use the information. Remember, user acceptance doesn't depend on how *you* perceive biometric authentication. Rather, it depends on how your employees perceive it.

Location

The geographic location of your facility plays a large role in the level of risk your business faces due to physical threats. Frequent storms, power outages, and a high crime rate are all examples of things to consider prior to selecting a location for your organization. Other issues include proximity to police and fire services. Quick reaction times associated with security events usually equate to reduced business impact.

Fire suppression

It might seem odd that a discussion of fire suppression systems occurs in a section on preventive controls. But consider that an effective fire suppression system can help prevent the destruction of your information infrastructure and, more importantly, injury to your employees.

A common type of fire suppression system is the ubiquitous fire extinguisher. Fire extinguishers are not intended to serve as your primary means of containing facility fires. Instead, their purpose is to assist in getting personnel out of affected areas. Mount extinguishers in plain view. Train one or more of your employees in their use. Quarterly inspections by a certified fire extinguisher servicing agency or company should be an essential part of your fire suppression strategy.

Another important consideration is the deployment of the proper types of extinguishers. For instance, the type of fire extinguisher you locate in your data center may not be appropriate for a manufacturing plant floor. Table 6-1 lists fire suppression system classes and the types of fires for which they're intended.

Class	Type of Fire	Suppression Agent
A	Ordinary combustibles (wood, paper, fabrics, rubber, plastics)	Water, soda acid
B	Flammable liquids (gasoline, oils, tar, paint, grease)	Gas (halon/halon substitutes), CO_2, soda acid
C	Electrical Equipment (computers, wiring, fuse boxes, etc.)	Gas (halon/halon substitutes), CO_2
D	Metals (magnesium, sodium, etc.)	Dry powder

Table 6 – 1: Fire Classes

We've established that fire extinguishers are not intended to actually suppress a large scale fire in your facility. That's the function of a fire suppression system integrated into your building's infrastructure. This type of system is designed to distribute a fire suppression agent over a large area. Two major types of systems that fall into this category are water and chemical.

Water systems are a good, inexpensive solution for areas where Class A fires are common. Your general office area is a good example. Water-based suppression systems can deliver water to a fire via standard sprinkler heads or by using deluge style heads. Deluge solutions deliver large amounts of water quickly. In addition to how the water is delivered, there are two approaches to how a suppression system stores water—wet pipe and dry pipe.

Wet pipe systems store water in the pipes feeding delivery heads. The advantage of this approach is the lack of delay in getting the water to where it's needed. The disadvantages associated with using wet pipe systems include:

1. Water freezing in the pipes if proper environmental controls are not used or available

2. Condensation build up causing water damage to computer equipment

Dry pipe systems help to solve these problems. In dry pipe systems, valves prevent the distribution of water into the pipes feeding distribution heads until a fire is actually detected. Upon detection of a fire, the valves open and water flows to the heads for release on the fire. This type of system is ideal in areas where pipes may freeze or in data centers where water damage from leaks or condensation may occur.

Although water-based systems are typically less expensive than chemical delivery systems, they are not the best choice for data centers. Aside from the fact that water delivered to extinguish a fire may cause more damage than the fire, there is the problem of false positives by your fire detection sensors.

More than once I've been involved in dealing with fires that didn't exist. Fire detectors are not infallible. In one instance Inergen, a chemical suppression agent, was delivered to my data center because two detectors under the raised floor interpreted a cooling unit gas leak as the presence of a fire. It took 14 hours to clean and bring the systems back to full production. If water had been delivered instead, it may have been necessary to transfer to our **hot site** until I could assess and replace my 250 servers, storage arrays, etc. If your budget requires the use of a water delivery system, consider the installation of a preaction solution.

Preaction water delivery solutions are very similar to dry pipe systems. The difference lies in what happens after the water is distributed to the distribution heads. In a preaction system, the suppression agent is not immediately released. For example, the actual presence of a specific level of heat might be necessary before water is actually delivered to affected areas. This provides time to take steps to cancel false alarms.

Chemical delivery systems are a much better choice to protect your data center. Since no water is released, there is little or no damage to critical systems. Recovery is faster, and the loss of critical data is minimized. Agents used in non-water systems commonly include FM-200, Inergen, and CO_2. The primary disadvantage associated with the implementation of a chemical-based system is cost. However, the additional cost provides the assurance of a reasonably quick recovery following a less than catastrophic fire.

Detective

The preventive physical controls we've discussed are not perfect; at some point, an intruder will successfully circumvent one or more of them. So let's look at some of the ways you can implement detective controls to support your perimeter defenses.

Detectors

Technology can play a large role in detecting whether an intruder has gained access to secure areas or areas peripheral to those areas. Examples include:

1. Light beams – A person or object moving through an area will break a beam of light passing between an emitter and receiver. When this occurs, an audible or silent alarm is initiated. Tools and techniques exist that allow intruders to detect and circumvent detection with a relatively low work factor.

2. Vibration/sound detector – These types of detection devices are often used to detect tampering with windows, doors, gates, or other barriers to entry. For example, a vibration detector might alarm with the breaking of a window. Mounting detectors to perimeter fencing is a common method for detecting intrusions as soon as someone enters your property.

3. Motion detector – Motion detectors serve a similar purpose to that of light beams. People or objects moving through an area are detected and alarms are initiated. Motion detectors might be more effective if you need to completely cover an area. Properly implemented, they should provide better overall security than light beam technology.

4. Closed Circuit TV (CCTV) – This control provides for continuous monitoring of perimeters and sensitive areas. However, it requires security personnel to watch for and react to incidents.

Guards

None of the detective controls listed above is effective unless coupled with human intervention. Immediate reaction depends on in-house security personnel. They can quickly assess and react to alarms or visually identified incidents. Whether or not you need your own security staff depends on two things—the level of risk associated with the compromise of your physical controls and the speed with which local authorities can respond to alarms.

Fire detection

Although I've separated our review of fire detection controls from that of fire prevention controls, both preventive and detective methods and technologies are required for effective fire prevention and control. There are two primary types of fire detection sensors: smoke and heat. Many "smoke" detectors are designed to detect any unusual gasses that might be caused by fires or heat. I prefer this type. Heat detectors might not initiate an alarm until a fire is well underway.

Detectors should be placed under your data center's raised floor, in the plenum space above the ceiling, and in air ducts.

LOGICAL/TECHNICAL CONTROLS

Logical controls, also called technical controls, are used to provide access to your organization's data in a manner that conforms to management policies. This includes the enforcement of the principles of least privilege and separation of duties. The following preventive and detective controls include both hardware and software.

Preventive

Preventive logical controls include the following:

1. Access control software
2. Malware solutions
3. Passwords
4. Security tokens
5. Biometrics

Access control software

Access control software, including operating systems (OS), control the sharing of data and programs through the enforcement of one of three access control methods: discretionary access control (DAC), non-

Access Controls

discretionary or role-based access control (RBAC), and mandatory access control (MAC).

DAC

DAC relies on the owner or creator of the data to apply security. An example of DAC is the use of folder and file permissions in Microsoft Windows. The owner/creator of a Windows folder or file can grant write, read, and execute permissions to the appropriate users. This might provide a quick and easy means of managing security, but this decentralized approach has disadvantages.

The major disadvantage is the lack of consistency in how access is granted to various classifications of information. Your organization must rely on each user's voluntary compliance with security policies to ensure assignment of the right levels of access.

RBAC

Access control based on role definitions is a much better approach when managing user accounts for a company with more than a handful of users. Roles, or jobs, within your organization are defined. Data owners then determine what access each of the roles should have based on data classification and security policies. There are two approaches to actually implementing the roles to control information access.

The high-end (translated expensive and resource intensive) solution involves the purchase and implementation of an identity management or account provisioning system. Such systems allow you to centrally manage user accounts and roles, including job transfers, hiring, password resets, and termination. Once the system is set up, simply add a user account to a role, and all necessary permissions are granted automatically. When she transfers to another job within your organization, the system automatically removes permissions associated with the old position and adds those required for the new position. Finally, stale accounts are prevented due to the automatic removal of all rights when an employee leaves your organization. Although the TCO for an account provisioning system is high, organizations that have to manage a large number of accounts might experience a ROSI rather quickly.

Another approach is the use of groups within your application or OS. In Windows, for example, the accepted practice for managing permissions with a RBAC approach is to create a group for each defined role. The group is then assigned permissions to network resources.

Just Enough Security

When a user is manually added to the group by your system administrator, he is automatically assigned all permissions assigned to the group. This function comes with the OS and with many applications. However, all hiring, transfer, and termination related activities must be managed manually.

MAC

MAC is the use of labels to determine the level of access required to access a resource and the potential level of access granted to each user. This is an access control approach that requires significant effort to implement and manage. The United States Government uses MAC to secure highly sensitive information.

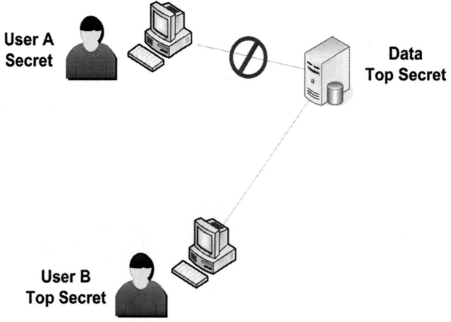

Figure 6 - 10: Mandatory Access Control

In Figure 6-10, the data the users want to access is labeled Top Secret. Based on organizational policies, User A has a classification of Secret and User B has a classification of Top Secret. The access control software compares the user classification, or label, to the data's label. If the user's classification is the same or higher than that of the data, and the user meets other requirements related to access, then the user is granted access to the data. In our example, User B is granted access

150

because her classification is the same as the data. User A is denied access because she has a lower classification. This is a simplified explanation of MAC, but you should get the idea.

Malware solutions

As we've seen in Chapter 2, malware is a huge threat, with the spread of spy-ware posing the largest risk to organizations and individuals today. The selection of an effective anti-malware solution is a critical logical control. Just as important is the need for larger organizations to implement a centrally managed solution. This helps ensure that all your systems run the most current version of your anti-malware software.

Passwords

The use of passwords is the most common preventive logical control in use. It's also the least effective. Using strong passwords to strengthen this control usually results in the opposite effect. Users post the password on their monitors, under their keyboards, or in other areas within their work area because strong passwords are easy to forget. If you rely on passwords, consider supplementing the password control with a second control, such as tokens or biometrics.

Security tokens

Used to authenticate a user to a system, tokens are hardware devices that can take the form of key fobs or credit cards. They are often used together with another logical access control, such as a password or pin, to implement strong multi-factor authentication.

Biometrics

We looked at biometrics in depth earlier in this chapter. Used in conjunction with a token, password, or pin, a biometric system can be a very strong logical access control.

Detection

There are two principle detection controls—audit trails and intrusion prevention/detection systems. System auditing creates a record of selected system activities. This record is written to disk in the form of a log that can be used to reconstruct a sequence of events. This is very useful in both determining if anomalous network behavior is indeed an attack and in confirming whether an employee performed unethical or illegal acts with company systems.

We've completed the basic areas into which access controls fall. But the critical access controls related to wireless networks, remote access, and firewalls deserve a more detailed look.

WIRELESS NETWORK ACCESS CONTROLS

The potential for unauthorized access to your company's network via wireless access points can be a big vulnerability. In this section, we'll discuss two controls to help you prevent both remote access and wireless intruders—IEEE 802.1x and RADIUS. Refer to Figure 6-11 for the following discussion.

802.1x is a standard protocol that controls who and what can connect to your network. When an end user device wants to connect to a network, it communicates with a portal device that serves as a RADIUS client. The RADIUS client blocks the device from connecting to the network and instead requests information with which it can authenticate the device or the user. In our example, the RADIUS client requires the user to enter her user ID and password.

Once the user enters the required information, the RADIUS client sends the information, along with an authentication request, to a RADIUS (Remote Authentication Dial In User Service) server. The RADIUS server uses the Network Security Database (Active Directory in the case of a Windows 2003 environment) to authenticate the user ID and password. If the authentication is successful, the RADIUS client "opens the door to the network," allowing the end user device to connect and the user to access authorized resources.

The 802.1x and RADIUS solution is effective for both remote access and wireless access control. In a wireless network, the RADIUS client is typically the wireless access point.

Access Controls

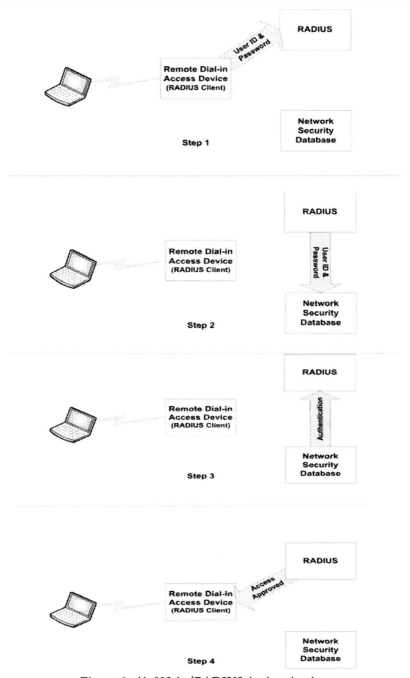

Figure 6 - 11: 802.1x/RADIUS Authentication

Just Enough Security

This process is a good way to keep unauthorized users off the network. But what about those drive-by hackers sitting in your parking lot capturing your sensitive data as it's transmitted from the end user device to the access point? There are two ways to deal with this problem.

Figure 6-12 depicts the first solution—encrypting the data as it moves back and forth between the end user device and the access point. Note that the data is encrypted only between the access point and the end user device. The two most commonly used wireless encryption standards are the Wired Equivalency Protocol (WEP) and Wi-FI Protected Access (WPA).

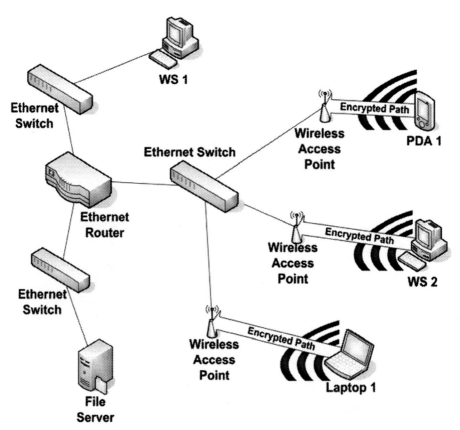

Figure 6 - 12: Access Point Encryption

WEP is the original wireless encryption algorithm. It's supported in both static mode and dynamic mode. In static mode, the key used by the access point and the end user device doesn't change. This presents a big opportunity for the hacker in your parking lot. Using any one of a number

Access Controls

of free tools downloaded from the Internet, he can crack the encryption and obtain your WEP key in less than twenty minutes. One of the reasons for the low work factor is a weakness in the WEP encryption algorithm.

In a dynamic WEP implementation, you can set the AP to automatically change the key on a regular cycle. By making the cycle time short enough, you can increase the hacker's work factor to the point where he might pack up and move to the parking lot down the street.

WPA doesn't suffer from the weaknesses of WEP. It ships with newer APs. In addition to supporting stronger encryption, WPA also uses the Temporal Key Integrity Protocol (TKIP) to change the key with each packet sent. This makes the packets much harder to crack. But there's a catch. The stronger encryption and the use of TKIP stress a system's processor and NIC. Performance may suffer. If you plan to use WPA, ensure your systems are robust enough to handle the additional processing load.

The second solution for wireless eavesdropping is VPN. Figure 6-13 shows an example of a wireless network implemented with IPSec VPN. A VPN tunnel is built between the wireless end user device and a device on the internal network. In our example, it's a file server. In most cases, the VPN termination point inside your network will be a router, a firewall, or a **VPN concentrator**.

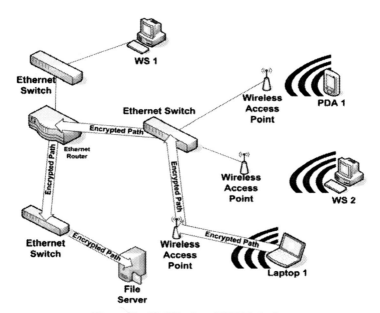

Figure 6 - 13: Wireless VPN Solution

> ### Key Terms
>
> **VPN Concentrator** – *A VPN concentrator is a device that is designed specifically to help build VPN tunnels.*

The big difference between AP encryption and a VPN is the portion of the data path over which the data is encrypted. In a VPN, the data is encrypted between the end user device and an internal VPN termination point. This is a good solution for highly sensitive date or if you are unable to implement something stronger than static WEP.

Another issue associated with wireless networks is the possible presence of rogue APs. A rogue AP is a device installed in your network without your knowledge or consent. One of your employees may install an AP to facilitate wireless access in a lab or conference room. If the AP conforms to your security policies, including encryption, this might not be so bad. But most rogue APs are simply plugged into an available network jack with no protection at all, creating a gaping hole in your wireless perimeter.

A worse scenario involves the intruder who surreptitiously enters your building, locates an unused but active network jack, and plugs in her own AP. If she hides the AP well, you may never know your perimeter has been compromised. So what can you do?

There are two solutions to this challenge. First, ensure that all unused network jacks are either disconnected from the network or are connected to an unused **VLAN**. Anyone connecting to the jack won't have access to any other devices. Second, implement a software solution that identifies the presence of rogue APs. Make sure your employees understand your policies pertaining to APs and the consequences of not adhering to them.

> ### Key Terms
>
> **VLAN** *(Virtual Local Area Network)* – *A VLAN provides additional flexibility to a network configuration. Using a sophisticated switch, a network administrator can combine several machines that might not be physically located together into a single broadcast domain. In other words, the devices in the same VLAN act as though they were connected to the same wire, even if on separate physical network segments. One advantage of VLANs is the option to move a machine from one physical location to another while keeping it on the same VLAN.*

Access Controls

Another consideration for minimizing wireless access threats is to make an attempt to hide the presence of your APs from the outside world. This can be done in three ways. The first method is to prevent your APs from broadcasting your wireless network SSID (Service Set Identifier). Each wireless network has an assigned SSID. By default, the SSID is broadcast in the clear to make it easier for authorized wireless end user devices to locate and use wireless service. But this provides an intruder with a beacon guiding him to your network. Although blocking the SSID broadcast is a good practice, this does not prevent someone from capturing the SSID as it's passed unencrypted between the access point and an authorized end user device during the initial connection process.

Second, consider turning down the power on your AP radios. Only use the amount of power necessary to cover your building. Also, place your APs to minimize the portion of the effective coverage area that extends beyond your building. Figure 6-14 shows how not to position an AP. Setting it in the window maximizes the extent to which the AP can communicate outside. A better location would be in the ceiling near an inside wall.

In some cases, you might not be able to reduce radio power or locate the AP in a more secure location because of coverage issues. The third method of hiding your APs, using directional antennas, helps meet these challenges. A directional antenna replaces the standard AP antenna. Once installed, you physically adjust the AP's coverage area by shifting the direction the antenna is facing. This provides for good coverage where you need it without serving the needs of crackers in your parking lot.

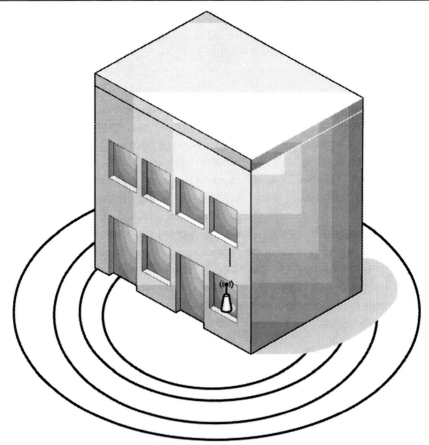

Figure 6 - 14: Locating an AP

REMOTE ACCESS

Most organizations today must provide remote access to customers and employees to remain competitive. Access from users outside your security perimeter may be accomplished via the Internet, direct dial-up, point-to-point T1s, or frame relay (see Chapters 2 and 4). But no matter how you provide access to external users, you should provide a layer of separation between them and your internal network. This layer of separation might simply take the form of a dial-up device configured as a RADIUS client or a set of firewalls configured as a **DMZ**.

A DMZ is a network segment located between external and internal firewalls. Devices between the two firewalls are accessible by the outside world, typically via the Internet. The purpose of the external firewall is

Access Controls

to filter packets to allow only traffic destined for the devices located in the DMZ. The internal firewall prevents any traffic from passing unless it consists of packets between one of the DMZ devices and a specific device on the internal network.

In the network depicted in Figure 6-15, traffic from users connected to the Internet can pass through the external firewall only if they are destined for one of the web servers in the DMZ, and only if seeking to connect to port 80 (standard web server service port). Once connected to one of the web servers, a user can use an application located on the server to request information from an associated database server within the internal network. Although the internal firewall won't allow the user direct access to either of the database servers, it will allow the application on the web server to communicate with the database servers, and obtain the information the user requested. Chapter 1 contains a more detailed description of how this process works.

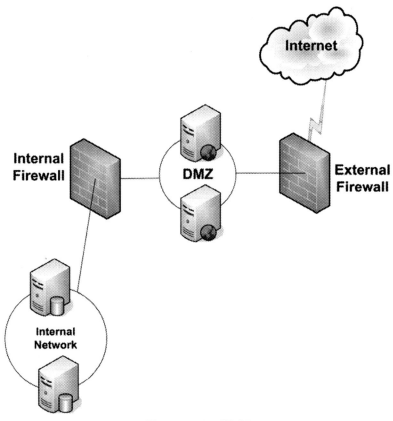

Figure 6 - 15: DMZ

You can also use firewalls to protect segments of your internal network. The following section explains the various ways firewalls work to protect your resources from unwanted guests.

Firewalls

We've discussed the use of firewalls in various parts of the book thus far. This section focuses on how firewalls work. As we've seen, firewalls provide protection against unwanted traffic from outside and inside your network. Three approaches taken by firewall vendors to provide this protection are static packet filtering, stateful packet inspection, and deep packet inspection. Firewalls are categorized based on their ability to perform one or more of these functions.

Static packet filtering

A device that provides static packet filtering services is considered a first generation firewall. Figure 6-16 provides an example of how this process works.

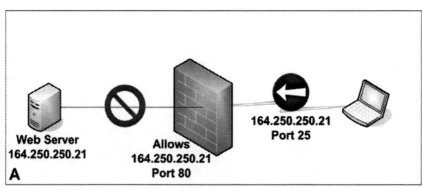

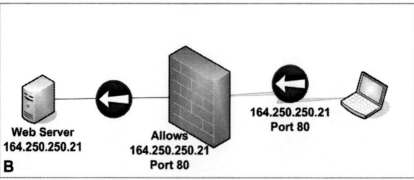

Figure 6 - 16: Static Packet Filtering

Access Controls

In Panel A, a remote workstation is attempting to access Port 25 on the web server, IP address 164.250.250.21. Port 25 is the default port for SMTP, a messaging protocol. The external firewall is configured to allow traffic for the web server only if it is destined for Port 80. Port 80 is the default web services port. When the workstation's packet reaches the firewall, the destination address and port are checked and compared to the list of allowed address/port combinations. Since it doesn't match, the packet is dropped (discarded); no communication takes place.

Panel B depicts a successful packet transmission. Unlike the packet in Panel A, the destination address and port match an address/port pair that is allowed to pass. The firewall sends the packet on to the network segment on which the web server is located.

As with stateful packet filtering and deep packet inspection, this process can be placed either at the perimeter of your network or at the entry point into a network segment containing sensitive data.

Stateful packet inspection (dynamic packet filtering)

Stateful packet inspection firewalls work in much the same way as static packet inspection devices. The primary difference lies in the stateful inspection device's ability to determine whether packets are parts of established sessions between devices on either side of the firewall.

For example, a stateful firewall device builds a state table to track each session initiated by a system on the internal network. Any traffic attempting to pass through the firewall into the protected network or segment is checked to see if it's associated with a session in the state table. If it isn't, the packet isn't allowed to pass. Another feature is the ability of a stateful firewall to dynamically open and close ports as they're needed by authorized sessions. Let's look at Figure 6-17 as we step through an example of how dynamic packet filtering works.

Two devices on the internal network have initiated sessions with devices on the Internet. These sessions are listed in the state table. 168.234.235.34 is connected to a SMTP service and 168.234.235.34 is connected to a web server. This is a scaled down version of a state table, but it's enough to represent stateful operation.

A device on the Internet attempts to send a packet to 168.234.235.34 with the intent of connecting to Microsoft SQL Server Port 1434. Although an address/port rule may not exist to block this packet, the fact that no system on the internal network is engaged in a Port 1434 session with an external device is enough to cause the firewall to drop the packet.

Just Enough Security

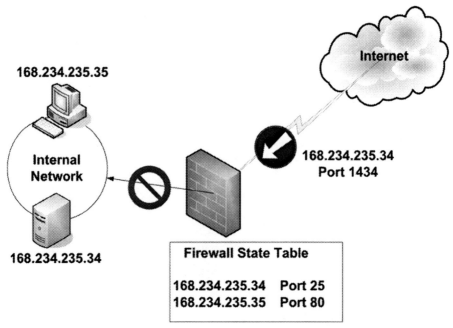

Figure 6 - 17: Stateful Packet Inspection

Deep packet inspection

Firewalls capable of deep packet inspection are the most sophisticated of the three types represented in this chapter. They are actually a combination of intrusion detection/prevention and stateful packet inspection services. We dig deeper into intrusion management technology in Chapter 7, but we'll take a quick look here at how this firewall technology works.

A deep packet inspection firewall actually looks at the payload or data section of a packet (see Chapter 1). It makes decisions about whether to pass the packet based on the contents of a state table or the contents of the payload.

The payload contents are inspected through signature matching, protocol anomaly checking, or with the use of heuristics. Signature matching is the process of comparing known malware or other attack patterns to the data contained in the payload. If there is a match, the packet is dropped. Anomaly checking is the process of comparing the packet format to what is expected based on the packet type and the protocol specified in the packet header. Heuristic algorithms are another way of determining if a payload contains unwanted data. But instead of trying to make a perfect match to a known attack signature, they make an

Access Controls

"educated guess" about the probability of the presence of hostile code in the payload contents.

Finally, behavior watching algorithms, concerned with the behavior of communication traffic rather than payload signatures, can also be employed by deep inspection firewalls. For example, they watch for PING sweeps, repeated attempts to connect to a port on the internal network, and other unusual network behavior to determine if an attack is underway.

Key Terms

PING sweep – *PING is the acronym for Packet INternet Groper. It's a TCP/IP utility typically used to determine if a specific IP address is active. For example, if a technician is troubleshooting network connectivity for a PC with IP address 192.168.125.32, she might enter the following at the command line of her PC:*

ping 192.168.125.32

If the troublesome PC is connected to the network and responding to packets sent to it, the technician would see the following:

Pinging 192.168.125.32 with 32 bytes of data:

Reply from 192.168.125.32: bytes=32 time=73ms TTL=243
Reply from 192.168.125.32: bytes=32 time=73ms TTL=243
Reply from 192.168.125.32: bytes=32 time=72ms TTL=243
Reply from 192.168.125.32: bytes=32 time=73ms TTL=243

Ping statistics for 192.168.125.32:
    Packets: Sent = 4, Received = 4, Lost = 0 (0% loss),
Approximate round trip times in milli-seconds:
    Minimum = 72ms, Maximum = 73ms, Average = 72ms

If the address is not active on the network, she would see the following on her screen:

Pinging 192.168.125.32 with 32 bytes of data:

Request timed out.
Request timed out.
Request timed out.
Request timed out.

> **Ping statistics for 192.168.125.32:**
>   **Packets: Sent = 4, Received = 0, Lost = 4 (100% loss),**
>
> *When an attacker wants to discover devices on your network, he might use the PING utility to step or "sweep" through a range of IP addresses he believes exists in your enterprise.*
>
> *Each time he receives the response above, he knows he's hit an active device. This type of activity is also performed by certain types of malware looking for more systems to infect.*

Regardless of what type of approach your firewall may use, when a possible attack is identified, the device can notify appropriate personnel, block the suspect traffic, or simply log the event. The choice as to how to handle an event is made by you or a member of your staff.

CHAPTER SUMMARY

Implementing the proper administrative, physical, and logical access controls is a key step in protecting your information assets. Controlling access to your infrastructure, employees, and data begins with developing the right policies and nurturing organizational awareness. This must be followed with standards and guidelines for controlling access to facilities and areas containing sensitive data. The access control loop is closed through the effective application of identification and authentication systems and methods designed to limit electronic access to critical or sensitive systems and data.

Knowing which access controls to implement and to what extent is a function of risk management, as covered in Chapter 3. Remember that risk management is concerned with more than just direct negative financial impact. It also takes into account regulatory constraints. In general, however, the degree to which management believes it must enforce separation of duties and least privilege for various data classification levels is a primary consideration for access control selection and implementation.

CHAPTER 7
INTRUSION DEFENSE

The various access controls we examined in the last chapter are effective, but not perfect. It takes more than a good password or physical security policy to deal with a determined intruder. Although building a fail-safe access control environment might seem like the ideal goal, I doubt if most organizations can afford to pursue it. In this chapter, you'll:

1. Learn about *deperimeterization* and the way it's changing how managers deploy security measures

2. Explore the need for *configuration management* and the activities necessary to protect your systems at the last line of defense

3. Learn how *intrusion detection systems* (IDS) work

4. Learn how *intrusion prevention systems* (IPS) protect your network and its connected systems

5. Learn how to use IPS and IDS as a *layered intrusion defense* solution

6. Learn why *spyware* is becoming a larger threat than the ubiquitous viruses and worms and how to protect your organization against infection

7. Examine how *personal firewalls* provide an additional layer of protection against unwanted visitors

THE NATURE OF THE THREAT

As we've seen in previous chapters, there are many threats to the confidentiality, integrity, and availability of your data. In this chapter, we'll look at these threats from two perspectives:

1. Inside threats caused primarily by disgruntled, financially stressed, or poorly trained employees
2. Outside threats consisting of malware on the Internet and for-profit human attackers

Ten years ago, protecting your network from attacks consisted of good access controls and a solid perimeter defense. Today this isn't enough. Malware comes in many new forms, and it's often unintentionally invited into your network by unsuspecting employees. Further, cracker attacks are shifting from an amusing pastime to a way to earn money—lots of it. Organized crime across the globe is cashing in on identity theft, corporate extortion, and corporate espionage enabled by weak information security practices. The perimeter defenses of yesterday are no match for today's attack vectors.

Deperimeterization

Deperimeterization is a relatively new concept that defines the nature of network security in today's information processing environment. Its basic premise is that the deployment of perimeter defenses alone is not a reasonable and appropriate approach to safeguarding your information assets.

Perimeter firewalls might be 100% successful in stopping external attacks if you closed all ports and allowed no traffic to pass, but this is impractical. It's a security best practice to open only those ports necessary to conduct business with your customers and business partners. This includes restricting port traffic to specific ports on specific IP addresses. However, attackers have developed ways to use these restricted paths to pass through your perimeter. And this isn't your greatest threat. Most attacks come from inside your network.

Laptops used by mobile users may become infected at some remote location. The infection is transferred to your network when the user returns to the office and connects the compromised device. Employees

Intrusion Defense

surfing the Internet unknowingly bring malware into your environment by visiting certain web sites or by downloading free software. And let's not forget email. Email messages are probably the most popular attack medium. Finally, the spread of handheld devices provides another way to circumvent your perimeter security. Your perimeter is no longer the high protective wall it once was.

In an effective deperimeterization model, network defenses are designed from the inside out. Figure 7-1 depicts a logical inside out design.

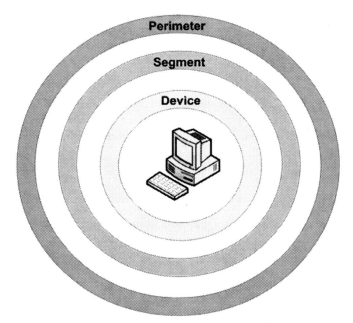

Figure 7 - 1: Layered Deperimeterization Defense

At the device layer, secure configuration and effective patch management processes, together with a host-based prevention solution, help protect against inside attacks that target a network segment. A segment layer defense consists of monitoring for and responding to attacks as the threat agent attempts to pass from one network segment to another. And a strong perimeter defense is necessary to help block and detect incoming malware or casual human attacks.

CONFIGURATION AND PATCH MANAGEMENT

An effective configuration management program is a key element in the protection of devices connected to your network. Attacks against your network are opportunistic. In other words, crackers are looking for soft targets, the compromise of which requires the lowest possible work factor. Properly configuring your applications, databases, and operating systems can increase the work factor so much that an attacker moves on.

Risks Associated with Poor Configuration Management

Poor, or nonexistent, configuration management practices result in network components that are easy targets. Some security risks include:

1. Known security flaws in operating systems, applications, and databases that are not patched. Potential attackers know about these vulnerabilities as soon as they're announced—often before they're announced. Failure to apply vendor-supplied patches to correct these flaws is an invitation to crackers looking for company networks where the vulnerabilities exist.

2. Unnecessary services running on workstations or servers.

3. Error messages that provide too much information. With the right tools, an attacker can intentionally cause an error on a network device. If the device is running with a default configuration, it might provide information about the operating system, system patch levels, etc.

4. Weak default passwords assigned to applications or system services. Accounts are sometimes created as part of the installation process for an application or operating system. Often the default password is easy to guess or doesn't exist at all.

5. Old production files or sample files left on server or workstation drives. Unused applications or demo software may leave behind scripts, applications, data files, configuration files, or web pages that may be easily exploited. You might not even be aware of their presence.

The purpose of configuration management is to effectively address these and other configuration issues in an effort to mitigate or remove vulnerabilities inherent in installed systems.

Building a Configuration Management Program

In the JES model, building a configuration management program to address the last two layers of the security model consists of the following steps:

1. Assign responsibility for managing and overseeing configuration management activities to a team or individual
2. Create secure system configuration standards and guidelines
3. Create and maintain an on-going configuration management process

Let's look at each of these steps in more detail.

Assign a responsible team or individual

Without assigning responsibility for creating and maintaining strong configuration management processes, your systems will most likely remain vulnerable to attack. Network engineers and software developers are usually very busy. Worrying about patches, unneeded services, and weak default passwords tend to fall low on the list of priorities. So who should be held accountable for proper device configuration?

In larger organizations, this responsibility often lies in Information Security. Information Security defines policies, standards, guidelines, and security baselines for enterprise systems, which are then used by engineering and development teams to design and implement business solutions. Information Security provides oversight by periodically testing installed systems for compliance.

In organizations without a dedicated Information Security team, I recommend assigning these tasks to the person or team responsible for managing the network. This separates vulnerability management from the person or team focused on implementing the organization's technology, and puts it into the hands of those individuals who perform day-to-day operational tasks. Day-to-day activities should be expanded to include not only definition of standards and guidelines but also oversight activities to ensure compliance.

Regardless of who's responsible, all members of your technical staff must work together to identify and remediate system weaknesses.

Create secure standards and guidelines

We examined the importance of policies, standards, and guidelines in Chapter 5. In this section, we focus specifically on the creation of secure baselines based on security program standards and guidelines.

Probably the most important task in configuration management is the creation of a security baseline configuration. This baseline configuration should be generic enough to allow its deployment on all workstations and servers, regardless of their use. In many organizations, multiple baselines may be necessary; workstations, application servers, and security servers may all require different baseline configurations. Applying the baseline to a workstation or server should accomplish the following:

1. All services not required for general operation of the device are disabled

2. All default accounts are disabled or controlled, and strong passwords are applied

3. Logging and alerting is enabled for failed logins, successful logins, and changes to security

4. All critical security patches are applied

Once the baseline configurations are created and tested, special purpose configurations should be created to enable secure operation of specific types of systems. These systems include, but are not limited to, email, database, and web servers. The application of a type-specific configuration should result in:

1. Necessary services, that might have been disabled with the baseline configuration, turned back on

2. Critical security patches applied to the applications running on the system

3. All default application accounts using controlled, strong passwords

Intrusion Defense

Upon completion of successful testing of the type-specific configurations, you're ready to deploy securely configured systems into your environment. Deployment consists of six steps.

1. Build a server or workstation using standard system build documentation
2. Apply your secure baseline configuration
3. Confirm proper configuration and operation of the system
4. Apply your type-specific configuration, if necessary
5. Confirm proper configuration and operation of the system
6. Move to production

Create and maintain an on-going configuration management process

It isn't enough to simply apply secure configurations and assume your network devices will remain secure. Configuration management is a continuous process that includes:

1. The creation and maintenance of a system inventory – It's impossible to develop an ongoing configuration management program unless you know, at a minimum, the operating systems and applications, with associated patch levels, that are running on your network.
2. Monitoring for the latest announced vulnerabilities related to the items in your inventory – The National Vulnerability Database (http://nvd.nist.gov/) and vendor sites are good sources for this information.
3. Prioritization of vulnerability remediation tasks – Not all vulnerabilities for which patches exist should be immediately patched. Managing the application of patches is a risk-based activity. A simple application of the risk management principles in Chapter 3 can help determine where to apply your resources to maximize your vulnerability mitigation efforts.
4. Testing of all configuration changes – Change management is a critical process in any configuration management program. Failure to properly test a change, and to assess the risks

associated with that change, might result in the same or greater negative business impact you would experience due to an attack.

5. Update baseline configurations, standards, and guidelines – Threats and vulnerabilities change over time. It's important to maintain a set of system configurations and processes that work to defend against the changing nature of system risks.

6. Continuous vulnerability scanning – There's always some drift from the optimum computing environment as defined in your security program. Vulnerability scanning, for both internal systems and of your perimeter, can help identify deviations from written policy. This prevents a false sense of security based on incorrect assumptions about the level of hardware and software compliance with security standards and guidelines. It also provides a means to determine how vulnerable your systems are to newly announced vulnerabilities.

Challenges to Effective Configuration Management

It isn't always easy to convince company management to commit resources to configuration management activities. Let's face it; there's no immediate positive impact on your company's bottom line. Other obstacles to effective configuration management include:

1. Lack of standard system configurations for workstations and servers – The greater the number of differences among your systems, the lower the probability that you'll be able to cost effectively manage system configurations. Testing for every possible combination of workstation and server image present on your network might require a resource commitment large enough to convince management to simply accept a large number of vulnerabilities.

2. Poor software quality or poor vendor response when vulnerabilities are discovered – When purchasing new solutions for your business, research the overall quality of each component. Include in your research the level of customer satisfaction with the component vendor's response to discovered security problems in their products. What is the average time between vulnerability discovery and patch release?

The proper application of risk management principles can help justify the additional effort required to select the right solutions and to manage inherent vulnerabilities over time.

INTRUSION DETECTION/PREVENTION

In the mid- to late 1990s, as attacks against corporate networks became a major concern, IT managers needed a way to determine if attacks were making it through their network perimeters. To meet this need, Intrusion Detection Systems (IDS) were developed. The purpose of an IDS is to monitor for intruder activity by looking at the following:

1. User activities
2. User policy violations
3. System integrity
4. File integrity
5. System vulnerabilities
6. System activities

There are two types of IDS: Network IDS (NIDS) and Host IDS (HIDS).

NIDS

A NIDS consists of sensors, or monitors, placed at strategic locations in a network. These sensors might send information about the network back to a central management system. When placed properly, a NIDS can provide visibility into all network activity.

Placement of sensors

Traditionally, NIDS sensors have not been fast enough to be placed inline. In other words, network traffic forced to flow through a NIDS on its way to a target device is likely to experience significant latency. So, NIDS sensors are typically connected to a network through the use of Switched Port Analyzer (SPAN) connections or taps. See Figure 7-2.

Just Enough Security

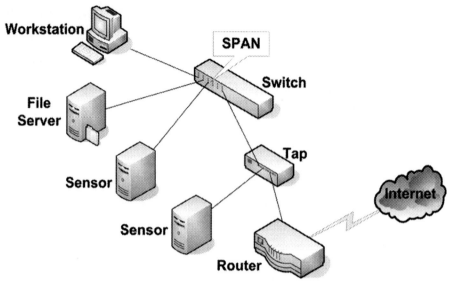

Figure 7 - 2: NIDS Sensor Placement

As you may recall from Chapter 1, a switch sends non-broadcast packets out of the port to which the target device is attached. If you simply plug a sensor into a switch port, or to a hub connected to the port, it will only see the packets sent out that port. It won't be able to see and analyze the packets traveling through the other ports in the switch. To correct this, you can configure one of the ports as a SPAN port. Copies of all packets traveling through the switch will be forwarded out of the SPAN port and available to the sensor.

A problem with SPAN ports is the possibility that the bandwidth of the configured port may not be sufficient to handle all the traffic passing through the switch. For example, if you are using a 24 port, 100 Mbps Ethernet switch, the SPAN port will likely be able to handle a maximum of 100 Mbps. So what happens if the other 23 ports are only 10% utilized? That's 230 Mbps of traffic attempting to squeeze through a 100 Mbps pipe. The switch is likely to drop packets, resulting in the sensor presenting an incomplete picture of switch traffic.

One solution to the bandwidth problem is the use of a 1 Gbps switch port as the SPAN port. Another solution is to configure multiple SPAN ports. Then aggregate data ports to each SPAN port in a way that guarantees sufficient bandwidth.

If you're only interested in analyzing packets passing through a single switch port, a tap might be the answer. A tap is a device placed inline with the packets you want to analyze. In a very simple implementation, a hub can be a tap. Since all packets entering a hub are sent out all the hub's ports, connecting a sensor to one of the ports results in all packets traveling to the sensor for analysis. The problem with using a hub is the lack of resiliency. If the hub in Figure 7-2 fails, all traffic traveling between the router and the switch will stop until the hub is repaired or replaced.

A device designed specifically to serve as a tap can provide the resiliency most business networks require. You can configure it to fail open. In other words, packets will continue to flow between the router and switch even if the tap fails.

Whether you use a tap or a SPAN port, you have to decide what it is you plan to monitor. Some placement ideas include:

1. Placing a sensor outside your perimeter firewall – This provides visibility into the types of attacks hitting your perimeter. An analysis of these attack characteristics can assist you in assessing and minimizing your vulnerabilities.

2. Placing a sensor in your DMZ – An analysis of traffic in your DMZ can help detect attack attempts that have penetrated the outer perimeter before they have the opportunity to gain access to your internal network.

3. Placing a sensor at the entrance to a network segment – It's a good idea to understand whether unusual traffic is moving in or out of the network segments that contain your most sensitive data.

Once you've placed your sensors, they can use signature detection, anomaly detection, or both to identify attacks against your information assets.

Signature detection

When using signature detection, a NIDS looks for byte patterns in packets or packet sequences that are common to known attacks. When there is a signature match, the NIDS logs the event. In most cases, companies set up the NIDS to send an alert when a possible attack is logged.

The key advantage of signature detection methods is the ease with which signatures can be developed if you know what you're looking for. In addition, signature detection might require less overhead on your monitoring devices; this depends on the number of signatures you want to analyze. NIDS vendors normally provide a means to select whether you want to check for all or just specific attacks.

Because signatures must be developed for each known attack, there is usually a delay between the time an attack is released into the wild and the time a signature is provided by your NIDS vendor. This is a disadvantage when defending against attacks during the first few hours or days after their release. Another disadvantage is the potential for a high number of false positives. A false positive results when a NIDS logs an attack, but an attack is not actually occurring. In many cases, signature patterns related to known attacks might appear regularly in perfectly normal traffic. Finally, in today's malware environment, threat agents, both human and malware, are capable of changing their characteristics both between and during attacks.

These disadvantages shouldn't stop you from deploying signature based detection methods. However, you should consider supplementing them with anomaly detection.

Anomaly detection

A NIDS using anomaly detection starts with a baseline of your network's behavior. Comparing later traffic to the baseline, the NIDS looks for statistical deviations from the network's normal operation. It also looks for unusual or incorrect packet configurations. Since anomaly detection methods are not dependent on attack signatures, they can detect attacks well before your NIDS or anti-malware vendors release an update to combat a new threat.

One disadvantage of anomaly detection is the difficulty often experienced in setting up rules the NIDS uses to assess what is and what is not characteristic of an attack. Although many devices are shipped with some predefined rules, it's rare that an organization implementing a NIDS doesn't have to tweak them a little. Each network is unique. To minimize false positives or false negatives, adjustments are usually necessary. Another disadvantage is the number of false negatives that can result when attacks do not cause a significant change to network behavior.

Intrusion Defense

If you decide to implement a NIDS, it's a good idea to consider using both detection methods to analyze network traffic. One method helps to mitigate the weaknesses in the other.

Active response

Current NIDS technology is capable of blocking attacks. One way to quickly react to detected attacks is to cause your NIDS to build packets intended to drop the connection over which the attack is occurring. Another method is to configure your NIDS to automatically reconfigure a router or firewall to prevent the flow of packets from the identified source of an attack. The advantage of using these methods is the elimination of the delay inherent in human reaction to NIDS attack alerts. This might reduce business impact, but crackers have figured out how to use these methods against you.

The right combination of specially formed packets sent by an attacker can cause your NIDS to view traffic coming from valid sources as attacks. If your NIDS is configured to do so, it will shut down all traffic associated with these sites; this effectively results in a denial of service attack. This doesn't mean you shouldn't consider using this technology; just be sure you understand its possible shortcomings.

So why use NIDS

Although NIDS may not be the best answer for preventing intrusions into your network, it can offer a low cost solution for identifying the who, what, when, where, and how of an attack. Armed with this information, you can take steps to either eliminate or mitigate the probability of another attack as well as the level of business impact. Two ways to accomplish this are sanctions and control modification.

As we discussed in Chapter 5, an effective security program includes well-defined sanctions and controls. Knowing who is responsible for intentional or unintentional network incidents allows you as a manager to deal with the human factor through additional training, counseling, or other more stringent means. Knowing what happened, when it happened, and how the attack was initiated can assist in strengthening the appropriate administrative, physical, or logical controls.

HIDS

Host-based intrusion detection operates on the same principles as NIDS. The primary differences are placement and scope of defense. A NIDS is placed in a strategic location on the network. It can therefore protect a large number of devices on the network or a network segment. A HIDS is placed on a specific computer. Its only purpose is to protect the host system on which it runs. Used together, NIDS and HIDS provide a multi-layer defense against attacks.

A host-based intrusion detection system is capable of performing several protective tasks. But since these tasks have been integrated into the more prevalent host-based intrusion prevention services, we'll not go into detail on the capabilities of HIDS in this book.

Problem with Intrusion Detection

Intrusion detection systems generate a huge amount of information about network activity. As we've seen, turning on automatic methods of stopping an attack can actually result in a self-imposed Denial of Service (DoS) situation. But manually reviewing this data to determine if an attack is underway is a very time-consuming task—and you don't really have the time. Today's attacks can travel across your network in seconds. Combining this challenge with the possibility of high rates of false positives and false negatives, intrusion detection has lost favor as a stand-alone weapon in intrusion defense.

INTRUSION PREVENTION

Intrusion prevention technology has the capability to detect attacks, both known and unknown, and to automatically prevent those attacks from resulting in a significant adverse impact on your business. As with intrusion detection, there are two primary deployment methods—network intrusion prevention systems (NIPS) and host-based intrusion prevention systems (HIPS).

NIPS

A NIPS device combines deep packet inspection technology with firewall traffic control functionality (covered in Chapter 6). Like a firewall, a NIPS is placed inline with the data. In the example depicted in Figure 7-3, all packets that pass to and from sources outside the perimeter are evaluated. All packets passing to and from *Segment B,* the home of the organization's most critical systems, are also checked.

Intrusion Defense

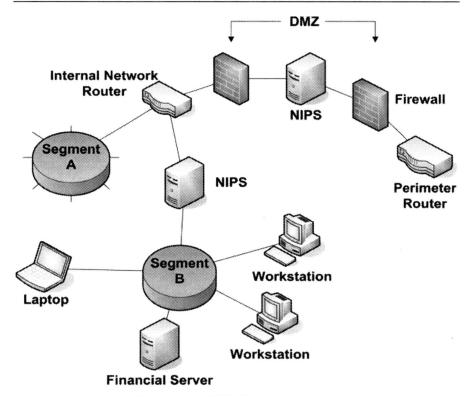

Figure 7 - 3: NIPS Device Placement

Through deep packet inspection, each packet is checked to see if it contains information that is indicative of an attack. Packets can also be evaluated in terms of open sessions. Any traffic that displays unusual behavior, or behavior that is clearly malicious, is immediately blocked by the NIPS.

When planning the purchase and implementation of a NIPS solution, you should consider the following:

Inline Operation – Inline operation provides for the discard of suspect packets. It also allows for blocking the remaining packet flow associated with the potential attack. Since it's inline, the NIPS is capable of stopping attacks without reconfiguring firewalls or routers. Inline operation of NIPS devices has been made possible by significant improvements in processing power.

Reliability and Availability – In order to provide continuous protection, the device you choose should function at a high level of performance with an acceptable mean time between failures (MTBF). You might also want to consider redundant devices so that if one fails, traffic will still flow through the other. In any case, if your inline device does fail, you want to ensure that the data continues to flow through the affected network segment. For example, if the NIPS protecting Segment B in Figure 7-3 fails closed, Segment B is effectively removed from the network. If the data on a segment is highly sensitive, you may want it isolated when no NIPS protection is available. In most cases, however, you'll want the capability of configuring the NIPS environment to allow the continuation of traffic in the event of a failure.

Accuracy – Ensure that the vendor from whom you purchase your solution provides regular detection updates. The application of these updates should be accomplished quickly with no interruption of information flow or protection. You should also check reliable third party sources to verify the vendor's claims about the rates at which false positives and false negatives occur. Finally, the device should be intelligent enough to thwart attempts by crackers to use its blocking capability to create a DoS attack.

Alerting and Analysis Capabilities – All information collected by the various NIPS placed around your network should be sent to a central console for evaluation. From this console, you should be able to run reports that provide information relative to investigations. The console application should also send alerts when an attack, or a potential attack condition, is recognized by one or more NIPS.

Highly Granular Configuration and Control Capabilities – When configuring and tuning your IPS devices, you should have the capability to define what attacks to detect and what policy violations to look for on specific network segments or on specific servers and workstations.

Adequate Level of Performance – Each NIPS should be powerful enough to assess network activity without hindering the flow of information across your network. In other words, they shouldn't create any bottlenecks. There should also be enough spare processing power in the devices to allow for growth during their life expectancy.

Proper placement of a NIPS can provide protection to a large number of network devices. In addition to servers and workstations, NIPS can protect firewalls, routers, VPN concentrators, etc.; it isn't platform dependent.

HIPS

Host-based intrusion prevention is designed to intercept and block attempts to perform behavior that is deemed prohibited or suspect by the business rules configured in your HIPS management system. It does this in two ways. First, it inspects all packets flowing in and out of a protected end user device or server. The methods used to inspect packets and network behavior at the system level are the same as those used by a NIPS solution—signature and anomaly recognition.

Second, it prevents one or more of the following activities associated with human or malware intrusions:

1. Copying files
2. Deleting files
3. Writing files to certain folders
4. Registry changes

The deployment considerations for HIPS are very similar to those listed earlier in this chapter for NIPS:

1. Reliability and availability
2. Accuracy
3. Alerting and analysis capabilities
4. Highly granular configuration and control capabilities
5. Adequate level of performance

In addition, HIPS must also:

1. Be capable of running your off-the-shelf applications when initially installed – Because a HIPS implementation blocks many activities on your workstations and servers, you must ensure that it doesn't prevent normal application execution.
2. Support user defined business rules and centralized device management – It isn't practical to attempt to manage hundreds of end user devices, for example, when rolling out new or modified

business rules. You should also have the capability of viewing alerts and system status from a central console.

HIPS deployment

HIPS is typically deployed as an *agent* on the device you want to protect. Your security team configures the agent through the use of centralized management software. Figure 7-4 shows the relationship between the management system and the agents.

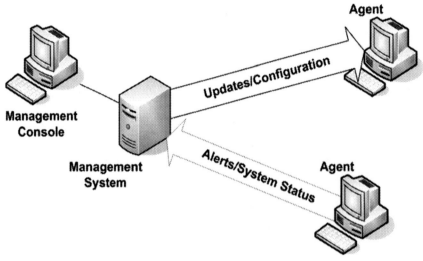

Figure 7 - 4: HIPS Management

Key Terms

Agent *– A small special purpose application that usually runs in the background.*

In this example, management software is running on a server. The person responsible for configuring and monitoring the HIPS environment accesses management functions via a management console. The management system sends business rules to the agents. These rules govern how the agents behave when dealing with activities on the systems where they reside. The agents send business rule violation alerts and system status back to the management system. This method of deployment allows an organization to effectively deploy HIPS to thousands of systems.

Intrusion Defense

HIPS vs. NIPS

We've seen that HIPS is very much like NIPS, so why even bother with the headaches of a device level implementation? Figure 7-5 helps answer this question.

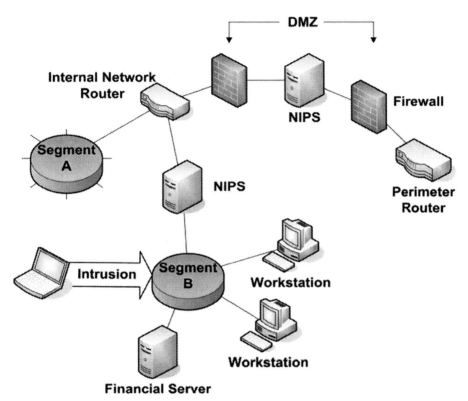

Figure 7 - 5: HIPS Protection

As in Figure 7-3, there are two NIPS devices in this network; one guards the DMZ and the other guards the door to Segment B. This is a very effective intrusion prevention solution for Segment B if all attacks come from other network segments or from outside the network. But what happens if an attack is initiated on a device connected to Segment B?

In Figure 7-5, a laptop connected to Segment B is infected with a worm. When the user of the laptop connects to the network, the worm seeks to infect other devices on the network. The NIPS protecting Segment B should protect the rest of the network from the activities necessary for the worm to propagate. But if the devices on segment B are not protected by HIPS, they are vulnerable to infection and possible compromise.

It might not be cost effective for an organization to install HIPS on every server and end user device. However, managers should consider purchasing HIPS licenses for their most critical systems. Further, if the laptop in Figure 7-5 was running HIPS, it probably wouldn't have served as an attack platform.

Benefits of a host-based approach

A NIPS is very effective at protecting against attacks directed toward your network, but HIPS goes one step further. It protects against system activities initiated by the attack. Roaming laptops are protected no matter where they connect. This not only protects the laptop information but it also helps prevent roaming systems from infecting your network when they return home.

A HIPS also protects against intentional and unintentional user activity. Configuring a HIPS agent to prevent copying, deleting, or writing files in a critical folder on an end user device can prevent many common support headaches.

Encrypted attacks are often missed by NIPS. HIPS solves this problem by inspecting traffic when it arrives at its destination and is decrypted. HIPS also makes up for an additional weakness in a NIPS environment by protecting against attacks from within a network segment.

It isn't necessary to place a HIPS agent on every device attached to your network. However, it's a good idea to deploy HIPS to those devices identified during your risk assessment as critical to business operation. Together with configuration and patch management, HIPS can supply the final line of defense against potentially damaging activities on your network.

IDS AND IPS AS A LAYERED DEFENSE

The implementation of IPS as a standalone intrusion defense solution may cause some problems for your IS staff and for your employees. When you deploy a NIPS, for example, you can usually use the default rules to block well-defined attack packets without much impact on your network. However, there are many attack types that will still get through. One way to deal with this is to purchase several NIPS, and configure

Intrusion Defense

them to block every conceivable attack. This might protect your network, but it might also stop some or all of your applications from working properly. A better solution is to partner a NIPS solution with NIDS. Figure 7-6 depicts this type of network configuration.

The layered configuration solution is very similar to the network depicted in Figure 7-5. In the previous example, a NIPS is placed in the DMZ to block packets with known malicious signatures and anomalous traffic. A second NIPS is placed at the entrance to a critical network segment. In Figure 7-6 I added a NIDS sensor to Segment A to watch for and alert on unusual network behavior. I could also remove the NIPS guarding Segment B if, by adding additional blocking rules, I cause the applications on that segment to fail. NIDS provides an organization with the ability to observe network traffic and react non-intrusively. You can build on the full network visibility of NIDS with the selective blocking capability of NIPS to create an effective intrusion defense and management program. Couple this with the protection provided by HIPS, and cracking your final defensive layers will require a work factor that only the most dedicated attackers will tackle.

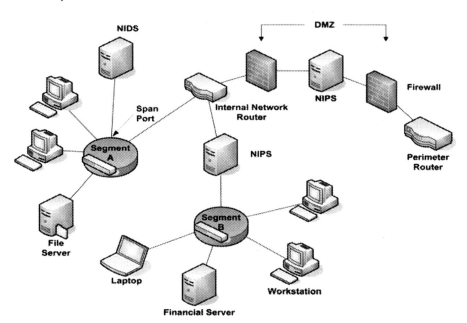

Figure 7 - 6: IPS/IDS Layered Intrusion Defense

Prior to designing your intrusion defense infrastructure, there are two more things to consider. First, although NIPS sensors can also serve in an intrusion detection role, deploying them for that purpose is typically not cost effective. Second, many current firewalls include IDS functionality, and many next generation firewalls include IPS functionality. You might be able to take advantage of this convergence of technologies to design a more efficient solution that easily fits within your security budget.

MALWARE DEFENSE

Crackers used to write malicious software (malware) for fun and to show off to other crackers. However, the reasons for intruding into corporate and personal systems have changed. Today, many crackers use their skills as a way to make money from illegal activities. These activities include:

1. Information warfare against governments
2. Extorting money from corporations
3. Identity theft

In many cases, the victims are unaware that their systems have been compromised. We examined how attackers use social engineering to surreptitiously gain access to your network in Chapter 2. In this chapter, we'll focus on how they might use malware to compromise your information assets.

Types of Malware
Malware exists in the wild in one of several forms. The most prevalent are:

Viruses – A virus is malware that an attacker attaches to another program you intentionally install or copy to your PC. When you run the wanted program, the malware also runs. Viruses can't propagate across the Internet or your network by themselves.

Worms – Worms are malware that can distribute themselves across your network and across the Internet. Once a worm takes up residence in a computer in your network, routines built into it attempt to locate other vulnerable systems by sending special packets over your network. Once a vulnerable system is found, the worm copies itself to that system. Now there are two copies of the worm attempting to propagate to devices in your processing environment. Over time, this replication process might slow network performance and compromise all vulnerable systems.

Trojans – A Trojan is a program that looks like a useful application. For example, you might download a free music player from an email advertisement. When you install the player, it performs as expected. But in the background, it's engaged in activities designed to compromise your system.

Spyware – Spyware is software you download and install, usually as part of another program installation, which gathers information about you, your company, and your system. It then transmits this information back to a parent system where a cracker is waiting to exploit it. Spyware is becoming such a major problem that the next section is dedicated to examining it in more detail.

Spyware

Spyware is quickly becoming the cracker's favorite tool for exploiting your data for profit. As we saw in the previous section, one of the primary means of delivering Spyware is to download software from the Internet. In many cases, the victim actually agrees to its installation along with the primary application. The victim is usually unaware of this agreement, because the spyware acceptance clause is buried several pages deep in the license agreement. Most business users either don't have the time to read the entire agreement, or they are unaware of the risks. But once they accept the agreement and download the software, their computers are compromised.

Another way spyware might be installed is through clicking "OK" on a dialog box that pops up when you visit a site. This can happen even if the dialog box is just informational. If you haven't blocked pop-ups on your employees' desktops, you should train your users to always click the "X" in the upper right hand corner of unexpected pop-ups. This will help prevent the unwanted installation of malware.

Once executing, spyware collects information about the user or about the system. Personal information that might be collected includes a user's Internet browsing habits, credit card numbers, and bank account information. Since spyware executes with the same security rights and permissions as the user, it can also access information stored in folders on the local machine as well as data in network storage areas.

After the information is collected, it is typically transmitted back to a host system managed by the individual or group who intends to use this information to steal the user's identity, blackmail her organization with threats of releasing sensitive information, etc.

Once spyware is installed on a computer, it can be very difficult to remove. In many cases, attempts at removal are reported back to the controlling system. The attacker can implement manual or automated processes to ensure that the application's components are reinstalled.

Attackers are increasingly using **root kit** technology to hide the presence of spyware on your systems. Neither the files on disk nor the processes running in memory are visible when using normal operating system tools or anti-spyware applications. Free utilities like *Rootkitrevealer* by Sysinternals (http://www.sysinternals.com/) can help locate and report on hidden spyware components.

Key Terms

Root kit — *A root kit is a set of applications that a cracker might install on a system he has compromised. It allows continued access to the system at the administrator, or root, level. Components associated with a root kit don't normally show up in directory listings or lists of running processes.*

Malware Prevention and Removal

The most important control in malware defense is to prevent malicious code from gaining a foothold in your network in the first place. Taking the following steps can help:

1. Keep all operating systems and applications updated (patches, service packs, etc.).

2. Properly adjust browser settings. The types of sites accessed and the types of Internet activities allowed have a direct impact on your organization's malware vulnerability. Web filtering software and pop-up blockers are a good place to start. A good web filtering solution:

    a. allows a manager to determine the types of sites the employees are allowed to browse.

b. is automatically updated, at least daily, with lists of sites that are known to spread malware. Blocking this web site category alone can significantly reduce business risk.

3. Use firewalls. How to detect and block malicious packets with Network firewalls is covered in Chapters 1 and 6. Later in this chapter, we'll look at how personal firewalls can add to the last layer of defense at the host level.

4. Implement strict system use policies and user awareness processes that cover:

   a. Downloading files from the Internet
   b. The importance of reading all warnings and agreements before installing downloaded software
   c. The dangers of installing anything that's advertised as free

5. Stress the importance of anti-virus and anti-spyware software on all systems attached to your network, AND KEEPING THEM UP TO DATE.

Even with all these controls in place, malware will eventually find a way into your network. So how do you detect it once it's made itself at home? First, all users, especially your company's help desk, should be trained to identify the signs of infection. They include:

1. The appearance of unexpected messages
2. The appearance of new tool bars or plug-ins
3. Programs starting by themselves
4. Systems running slower than normal
5. Browser settings changing automatically
6. Systems suddenly rebooting for no reason or after unusual warning messages are displayed
7. Any strange, unexplainable system activity

Second, updated anti-virus and anti-spyware software should detect and remove all non-hidden malware components. Finally, an organization's defense should include personal firewall or HIPS solutions. These solutions may not remove the threat, but they can prevent or delay activities initiated by the threat until your response team can contain and eradicate it.

PERSONAL FIREWALLS

Personal firewall technology is more mature than HIPS. Its use is a popular and effective way to protect both mobile and stationary users from becoming infected or infecting your network. Its functionality in preventing malicious activity targeted at both the host system and the organization's network position it as an alternative to HIPS as a last line of defense.

A personal firewall is traditionally an application that is installed on an end-user device. Once installed, it performs several protective functions, including:

1. Permitting or denying communication, both outgoing and incoming, based on one or more user-defined policies
2. Helping to protect laptops when connected to other networks and protecting the parent network from infection once the laptop returns home
3. Prompting a user to accept or reject a process request to perform an action that violates one or more policies
4. Helping to prevent self-imposed DoS by blocking specific types of traffic, both outgoing and incoming
5. Providing some level of HIDS by logging unusual system behavior
6. Helping to identify attacks coming from internal sources

Because of the growing necessity for the presence of personal firewalls on end-user devices, most of the anti-virus vendors include personal firewall technology in their basic offerings. But like any protective technology, there are challenges associated with implementing them.

1. Personal firewalls consume system resources. Make sure your end-user devices have the memory and processor resources necessary.

2. Attackers have developed ways to compromise personal firewalls without your knowledge. The presence of a personal firewall might result in a false sense of security.

3. Rolling out personal firewalls to a large number of devices, and managing them once installed, can be a daunting task. Like HIPS implementations, personal firewalls should be managed by centralized software. This provides for:

    a. Application of software updates

    b. Ensuring firewalls are running on each end-user device

    c. Easy roll-out of attack signature or anomaly detection information

    d. Management of how your users interact with the firewall—this includes allowing or disallowing them to take an action the firewall warns them against

4. Ensure that your host-based applications will continue to run once the firewall is operational.

We've examined both personal firewalls and HIPS. So which is better? The answer is, "it depends." HIPS is an emerging technology. As such, it has some issues that need to be worked out. Personal firewall technology, on the other hand, is mature and mainstream. Which of these solutions you decide to use depends on your organization's willingness to accept and deploy new technology. If your company is technically conservative, or you haven't the time to deal with the growing pains of HIPS, I recommend the safe personal firewall route. Which technology you pick is less important than ensuring that this final layer of intrusion defense is not ignored.

CHAPTER SUMMARY

Deperimeterization has strengthened the need for multiple layers of intrusion defense. The use of IDS and IPS, both network and host, helps in this effort. Both external and internal threats can be detected, stopped, or delayed by the proper placement of sensors.

Configuration management is a key component of intrusion defense. Hardening workstations and servers with secure operating system and application settings, together with effective patch management, minimizes the impact of attacks that make it through all other layers of your security infrastructure.

Malware is a significant threat to organizations. Implementing protection against the growth of spyware attacks is probably the most critical step a business manager can take when considering malware defense strategies.

Finally, personal firewalls can provide a solid last line of defense, even when your patch management processes fail to keep up with the daily discoveries of new vulnerabilities.

Part 3
Continuity Management

CHAPTER 8
BUSINESS CONTINUITY PLANNING

In Part II, we explored the various elements of the JES layered security model. In Part III, we examine two activities that help to manage and maintain the availability and integrity of all the components of your information processing environment in a way that maximizes up time and minimizes customer and employee frustration. The first of these activities is ensuring Business Continuity Planning. In this chapter, you'll:

1. Learn about why *Business Continuity Planning* is critical to maintaining uninterrupted service and product delivery to your customers

2. Examine the *five phases* required to develop and maintain effective recovery plans

3. Learn the key principles involved in *testing* your plans and *preparing your recovery teams*

WHAT IS BUSINESS CONTINUITY PLANNING

The purpose of Business Continuity Planning (BCP) is to ensure the uninterrupted delivery of products and services to your customers. In essence, its goal is to help you perform your daily operations in order to stay in business by preventing:

1. Loss of business to competitors
2. Supply chain interruptions
3. Injury to customers or employees
4. Loss of reputation

Many people think of BCP as synonymous with Disaster Recovery Planning (DRP). Although DRP is important, it's only one piece of effective BCP. The probability that your business will suffer a catastrophic event is much less than the probability of experiencing a failed server or router. BCP should be integrated into all business processes; it should be a standard part of any technology project or implementation plan. So how does an organization achieve a reasonable and appropriate level of business continuity assurance? The rest of this chapter is focused on answering that question.

The Five Phases to Business Continuity Assurance

In the JES Security Model, achieving business continuity assurance is accomplished through a 5-phase process, depicted in Figure 8-1.

Figure 8 - 1: Five Steps to Business Continuity Assurance

Phase I: Analyze

The purpose of the first phase is to analyze your business. This goes far beyond a simple analysis of your network infrastructure. It also includes the following:

1. An understanding of all processes that make your business function – This must also include how those processes work together to produce business outcomes.

2. The identification of vendors and other business partners whose contributions to your operation are critical for product and service delivery –Include why and in it what manner you interact with each entity. It's also important to record contact information as well as the existence of agreements that contain clauses dealing with interruption of deliveries, service, support, payments, etc.

3. A thorough understanding of your information processing infrastructure – It isn't enough to understand your internal network; you must also understand how your network interfaces with the networks of your customers, banks, and suppliers. Your infrastructure assessment must include all required workstations, servers, storage devices, backup/restore systems, and communication services.

4. An understanding of which people are critical to your business – These individuals are often not on your management team. Rather, they are the people who work in the trenches every day. Their understanding of how to get work done is a key element to maintaining business continuity. Additional information about them, and the tasks they perform, includes:

    a. The existence of cross-training to ensure more than one person can adequately perform business critical tasks

    b. An assessment of how to maintain business continuity if key people are unable or unwilling to participate in recovery operations

    c. The identification of vendors who will assist with your recovery – They might include:

        - Computer hardware and software vendors
        - Recovery site vendors
        - Communication vendors

d. The creation of a contact list including all key employees – Contact information should include:

- Home address
- Home phone
- Cell phone
- An assessment of all key support services, including:
- Email
- Voice communication
- Fax services
- Mail
- Shipping and receiving

Upon completion of the analysis phase, you should have a clear view into the people, processes, and technologies necessary to continue delivering products and services. As we move to the next step in the BCP process, we'll begin to assess the risk associated with the full or partial loss of one or more of them.

Phase II: Assess Risks

Conducting a BCP risk assessment follows the same steps as those defined in Chapter 3. So in this chapter, we'll focus on the specifics of conducting a risk assessment as a component of continuity planning.

Once you complete Phase I, you should have a well-defined list of critical people, processes, and technologies. As the first step in a BCP risk assessment, you need to identify the internal and external threats. Next, you need to look at the critical components of your organization to determine the vulnerabilities of each to the identified threats. Finally, the business impact of the partial or complete loss of each critical operational component must be determined. Some of the areas you should address include:

1. Loss of short term revenue
2. Loss of long term revenue
3. Loss of investor confidence
4. Loss of key employees
5. Loss of facilities or other key fixed assets

As you work through these and other possible adverse impacts on your business, try to change a limited set of variables through the use of scenario planning. During the process of scenario planning, management and key employees can work through several kinds of business continuity interruptions. This can help determine if the BCP team has considered all critical recovery requirements. Your list of scenarios might include:

1. One or more facilities are untenable, but the information processing infrastructure is still operational. This could be caused by:
    a. Chemical spills
    b. Blizzard
    c. Floods
2. One or more facilities no longer exist due to fire, hurricane, explosion, etc.
3. All facilities are operational, but a supplier is temporarily shut down due to a catastrophic event.
4. The central data center is no longer operational, but all other facility functions are capable of normal operation.
5. In the case of a catastrophic event, many key employees or their families are affected. This results in one or more critical employees being unable or unwilling to help with your recovery efforts. According to Burtles (2004), the following questions should be answered as part of continuity planning:
    a. Who is prepared to do what? What activities and conditions will they tolerate?
    b. Who is not prepared to do certain things?

c. What are the general reservations, or things the entire team is reluctant to do?

d. List what people can do above and beyond their normal duties. For example, who may have a 4-wheel drive vehicle or unique skills other than those used daily at the office?

Using the results of the scenario planning activities, build a quantitative or qualitative risk assessment chart as depicted in Chapter 3. The resulting risk scores will help with prioritization of process recovery during Phase III.

Finally, a list of all key processes should be placed in a matrix that includes, at a minimum, the following information:

1. The process owners
2. Key individuals required to produce the desired outcomes from each process
3. The technology required to execute each process and any manual tasks that may be used as workarounds
4. The maximum number of hours or days the organization can survive without the output of each process
5. Any special considerations resulting from the scenario planning activities
6. Dependencies (what processes must be operational to support one or more other processes)

After compiling all assessment information, you're ready to begin developing a recovery strategy and plan.

Phase III: Strategy and Plan Development

Prior to developing your recovery plan, review the risk assessment matrix to select the appropriate business continuity strategy for each risk. It's important to understand that the strategies you develop for each system directly impact recovery planning. As you might recall from Chapter 3, the possible strategies are:

Business Continuity Planning

1. Accept the risk
2. Transfer the risk
3. Reduce or eliminate the risk

Accepting the risk means taking no steps to prevent a security event caused by the exploitation of a specific threat. However, planning should include clear recovery steps to minimize business interruptions through quick, efficient recovery activities. Transferring the risk includes purchasing business interruption insurance. However, it's important not to be too short-sighted. Your insurance carrier might pay for short-term losses, but you may never recover from the long term effects due to the loss of customer or investor confidence. Reducing or eliminating risk is typically accomplished by reducing or eliminating vulnerabilities. Business continuity vulnerabilities might include:

1. A single point of failure, such as a server, router, switch, or firewall
2. Lack of proper documentation on how to rebuild one or more components of a system
3. Insufficient skills within the technical teams to quickly recover from system failures
4. Lack of agreements with vendors that obligate them to respond quickly if one or more system components fail
5. Lack of an overall technical recovery plan, or the presence of an untested recovery plan
6. Lack of documented manual processes that can be initiated if one or more system components fail
7. Lack of cross-training programs to ensure that more than one person possesses a critical skill set
8. Non-IS personnel are not involved in recovery testing

Strategies for dealing with these and other potential vulnerabilities can take many forms. For example, single point of failure vulnerabilities can be reduced by maintaining one or more duplicate components "on the shelf." This helps reduce downtime by eliminating equipment acquisition time. Another method is to implement redundant components. This provides for minimal downtime through automatic fail-over from a malfunctioning device to one that is either on standby or load balanced with the failed component. Another important way to mitigate risk is to include the proper maintenance of system build documentation in all project plans. Whatever the vulnerability you might identify, ensure you mitigate it to the point where you can recover each system before the **maximum tolerable downtime** (MTD) is reached.

> ### *Key Terms*
>
> ***Maximum Tolerable Downtime (MTD)*** *– MTD is the period during which a specific business process can be down without significant business impact. Every effort should be made to ensure that a process is recovered prior to exceeding its MTD.*

Now that the risks are identified, and you've documented strategies for dealing with them, you're ready to build your recovery plans. The following are some recommended steps to creating a successful recovery plan:

1. **Create a clear communication plan.** When a business continuity event occurs, communication is probably the most important recovery activity. All stakeholders must be kept informed of the type of event, the impact on the business overall, and the impact on their teams or departments. Understanding the scope of an event helps managers determine the best courses of action to maintain the critical processes for which they're responsible. Other points of contact should include:
    a. Fire services
    b. Law enforcement services
    c. Shareholders
    d. Press
    e. Customers
    f. Your insurance company
    g. Vendors

As you can see from the list, some communication is necessary to manage damage to reputation and public confidence as well as to mitigate internal business operations.

2. **Create recovery teams.** Taking a look at your recovery requirements, create a team for each specific recovery area. For example, select a team of individuals who will travel to your **hot site** to rebuild your data center. Another team you might consider is a group of individuals assigned to set up a temporary office environment with phones, workstations, fax machines, and other office equipment necessary to perform day-to-day activities.

    This is in no way a comprehensive list. The teams you create for your organization will be unique to your recovery requirements. How to staff and train recovery teams is examined in Chapter 9.

3. **Create easy to follow checklists.** When first responding to a business continuity incident, your response teams shouldn't be encumbered with lengthy, verbose technical or process documentation. Rather, they should follow checklists that quickly guide them through the initial stages of the recovery process. Reacting quickly during the first few hours of an incident is critical to positioning your organization for a successful recovery. Completion of the checklists should result in:

    a. Notification of critical personnel

    b. Identification of the type of incident

    c. Identification of the scope of the incident

    d. Mitigation of business impact

    e. Initiation of process and technology recovery efforts, if necessary

    The checklists should only include those activities that require *immediate* attention. As with all BCP documentation, involve your teams in the creation of the checklists.

4. **Create system/process recovery documentation.** In addition to lists of forms and other items necessary to implement

temporary manual processes, this step requires the creation of detailed documentation that results in the recovery of all delivery systems. Examples include:

    a. Server and workstation build documents

    b. Application and data recovery documents

    c. Manual process instruction documents

5. **Plan for worst-case scenarios.** Creating documentation for each possible scenario might not be practical. Your business continuity teams are typically engaged in day-to-day operational activities when they're not working on BCP activities. In such cases, develop all recovery documentation with the intent to recover from catastrophic events. If your teams are properly trained, they should be able to adapt the plans to lesser incidents. Regular testing will help to develop the necessary awareness and flexibility.

Phase IV: Test the Plan

Testing the plan is probably the most important part of BCP, and it's often the most neglected. Organizations that fail to conduct regular tests can't reasonably expect their recovery teams to react quickly enough to an actual incident.

> *"The true measure of success from a business perspective is the pace of recovery. All of our business continuity plans and preparations are aimed at improving response and recovery times in order to reduce the impact on the business"* (Burtles, 2004).

To reach the measure of success defined by Burtles, your testing must target two primary objectives. First, your teams must be so familiar with the recovery process that management intervention is unnecessary except to help teams overcome external obstacles. Second, all inaccuracies in the documentation should be identified and corrected. This includes inaccuracies caused by mistakes or by changes in the business environment. It's also a good idea to question all recovery activities. Do they represent the most efficient path to recovery?

Testing should be a multi-step process. Without proper preparation, BCP tests will fall far short of your objectives. Successful testing consists of three steps - educate, maintain, and test.

Educate

Each team must be educated on the contents of the documents related to their areas of responsibility. Team education should result in:

1. An understanding of team roles
2. Solid knowledge of the processes and steps contained in the documentation
3. Elimination of team member resistance and apathy – In many organizations, the initial reaction to business continuity activities is that they are a waste of time—things that pull them away from "real work." The education process must address this issue by helping team members understand the importance of BCP.
4. Recommendations from the teams on how to improve the recovery processes
5. Team leaders having a high level view about how their teams' activities fit into the overall recovery plan

Maintain

Between tests, the documentation must be properly maintained. The best way to accomplish this is through an effective change management process. Some of the deliverables of change management are updated configuration and build documentation for infrastructure components, updated process diagrams, and changes to forms required for manual processes. The responsibility for ensuring that documentation changes are made and included in the BCP must be clearly defined.

Test

The purpose of testing is to ensure that the documentation is accurate and to increase the awareness of recovery teams. Other reasons to test include:

1. Recording system recovery times

2. Identifying and documenting system recovery dependencies – In some cases, systems must be recovered in a specific order to fully recover delivery systems.

Once you're confident that your documentation is reasonably accurate, plan for the test. You don't have to successfully restore a system to have a successful test. Remember, testing is designed to raise the awareness of your teams and to identify inaccuracies and inefficiencies in your documentation. However, you should establish certain guidelines and test objectives for each test. The following steps will help with the test planning process:

1. **Establish a test strategy.** This should include the type of test and the systems and processes you want to recover. There are three basic types of tests—checklist, walk-through, and hot site. A checklist test is performed by the individuals in your organization most familiar with the process or system being tested. The purpose of this test is to ensure the accuracy of the documentation. A walk-through is typically performed by one or more recovery teams sitting at a conference table. Walking through the recovery documents as though they were actually recovering from an incident increases awareness and helps identify roadblocks to recovery. A hot site test is an actual physical build of infrastructure and business processes.

2. **Clearly define the objectives of the test.** Often, the objective of a test may be to simply test how long it takes to recover one or more systems. Other times, you may need to demonstrate that you can recover and run a specific task. For example, your objective may be to recover your payroll system and actually print checks. Whatever your objectives, everyone participating in the test should understand what it is they're trying to accomplish.

3. **Define how the test is to be conducted.** Part of test planning should include criteria governing how the test will be performed. This includes how the documentation should be used, the types of logs and reports each team must complete, and the sequence of events. One challenge you should address is the tendency for teams to recover processes and systems based on memory rather than using the recovery documentation. This is usually a bad

idea. Planning for worst case scenarios includes planning for recovery situations in which your internal staff might not be available. If the documentation is not tested through strict adherence to it during recovery tests, you probably won't be able to rely on it in an actual declared disaster.

4. **Select test team.** Selecting the team for the test is relatively easy. The team responsible for the process or technology being tested should conduct the test. Ensure that each member of the team understands the test strategy, objectives, and how the test is to be conducted.

5. **Test.** Step through each phase of recovery, including initial notification of team members, immediate response through checklist implementation, and full system/process recovery. During the test, the following items should be documented in detail:

    a. Test start time

    b. Time each task in the plan is completed

    c. Actual time to complete each task

    d. Inaccuracies encountered in the documentation

    e. Recommendations for improving response and recovery times

Phase V: Manage Test Results

Using the documentation generated during the test, conduct an After Action Review (described in Chapter 9). The fundamental purpose of the AAR is to identify and address people, process, and technology issues related to efficient and effective recovery. The output of the AAR is an action plan that, at a minimum, should include the following activities:

1. Documentation updates

2. Modifications to agreements with recovery vendors

3. Changes to processes

4. Team restructuring

The results of the test, including the AAR action plan, should be communicated to management as soon as possible after the test.

The BCP produced by Phases I through III is not just a book for the auditors that sits unused on someone's bookshelf. Regular testing followed by a remediation action plan, Phases IV and V, is the cornerstone of an effective business continuity program. This is an incremental, evolving process. Each time you execute the test-manage cycle, your team becomes a little more capable of responding to business continuity events in a way that prevents significant business impact.

CHAPTER SUMMARY

Business Continuity Planning is an essential part of ensuring the uninterrupted delivery of products and services. There are five phases to business continuity assurance—analyze your business, assess risks, develop a strategy and plan, test the plan, and manage the results.

Business Continuity Planning is not a one-time project. It is a continuous process that results in incremental improvements in your organization's ability to effectively recover from unplanned business interruptions.

Works Cited in Chapter 8

Burtles, J. (2004, June). Beware the complex plan. *Continuity Central.* Retrieved November 13, 2005 from http://www.continuitycentral.com/feature097.htm.

CHAPTER 9
INCIDENT MANAGEMENT

In this chapter, we'll examine how to prepare for and respond to security incidents. Although Business Continuity events are technically security incidents, BCP was covered in sufficient detail in Chapter 8. While the focus of this chapter is responding to human and technical attacks against your network, the topics related to building and training an Incident Response Team are also relevant to business continuity planning and testing. In the following sections, you'll:

1. Learn why *Incident Management* should be a critical part of your security efforts
2. Examine the steps necessary to build an effective *Incident Response* capability
3. Learn how to *contain* and *eradicate* threats
4. Explore the path to *recovery* after an incident occurs
5. Understand the steps necessary to strengthen your security safeguards to mitigate or eliminate business impact from like incidents in the future

THE PURPOSE OF INCIDENT MANAGEMENT

Once a security incident occurs, it's management's responsibility to minimize loss and destruction. According to NIST SP 800-58, "An incident can be thought of as a violation or eminent threat of violation of computer security policies, acceptable use policies, or standard security practices" (Grance, Kent, & Kim, 2004, p.2–1).

An eminent threat is defined as a reasonable belief, based on information received, that an incident is about to occur.

When responding to an incident, the first consideration is protection of human life. The second consideration is the restoration of information processing services. The final consideration is mitigation of weaknesses that might have been exploited during the incident. An Incident Management program that effectively addresses these areas will produce the following benefits for your organization:

1. The business impact of each incident is minimized
2. The safety of your employees is enhanced
3. Corporate liability due to lack of due diligence is mitigated
4. Regulatory requirements are met
5. Your organization's public image is protected by a fast, professional response

THE PATH TO EFFECTIVE INCIDENT MANAGEMENT

In Chapter 2, I introduced a simple four-step process for addressing incidents. In this chapter, we'll expand that process, as depicted in Figure 9-1.

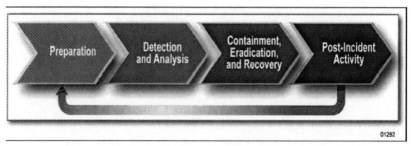

Figure 9 - 1: Incident Management Process (Grance, Kent, & Kim, 2004, p. 3-1)

Incident Management

The center two steps of this process map to Figure 2-10 as shown in the table below.

Figure 2-10	Figure 9-1
Identify	Detection and Analysis
Contain	Containment, Eradication, and Recovery
Eradicate	Containment, Eradication, and Recovery
Control	Post-Incident Activity

Figure 9 - 2: Process Comparison

Expanding on Figure 2-10, I've added preparation as a first step to be taken prior to the occurrence of an incident. I've also included additional activities in the Control phase. Let's walk through the process.

Preparation

Before an incident occurs in your environment, it's important to do everything you reasonably can to prepare yourself for a quick and effective response. The steps leading to the proper preparation of your organization include:

1. Developing an incident management policy
2. Forming and training incident response teams
3. Developing a communication plan

Develop an incident management policy

The first step in any security activity is the creation of a policy that clearly states your objectives. You should include:

1. A statement of management commitment to an effective incident management capability
2. Purpose
3. The business and security objectives to be met
4. A statement defining how your organization defines a security incident
5. An incident management and response organization structure

The organization structure section of the policy is very important. Each person in your company responsible for incident response must clearly understand her role and the roles of other teams with which she'll have to interface. The lack of a clearly defined organization structure can create confusion resulting in each phase of a response taking longer than necessary. This almost always leads to a more severe impact on your business. Some things to consider when planning your incident management teams include:

1. The role of each team
2. Clearly defined responsibilities assigned to each team
3. Levels of authority – The chain of command, leading up to a single recovery manager, should be easy to follow. Further, the incident response teams should be given sufficient authority to make decisions necessary to shut down or confiscate systems to protect your information assets.
4. Prioritization of incidents – Various types of incidents will occur in your organization. Each type might require a unique response with specific reporting requirements.
5. An explanation of reporting requirements – What is each team's responsibility for reporting, what should be included in the reports, and to whom are the reports submitted?

This policy forms the foundation for the next two steps in incident management preparation.

Form one or more incident response teams

Cross-functional Incident Response Teams (IRTs) are your basic weapons against all types of incidents. The proper staffing and training of these teams is critical to your recovery success. Whether you need one or ten teams depends on your business environment. In any case, each team should consist of the following:

1. A team manager – This person has an overall responsibility to ensure business objectives are met during an incident response activity. In addition, she's responsible for communicating status to senior management.

2. A technical lead – The technical lead is charged with assessing the scope of the impact of an incident on the technology infrastructure. He's also responsible for containment and recovery activities as they relate to information processing systems. The technical lead supervises the following members of the IRT:

   a. One or more network engineers
   b. One or more programmers
   c. Public relations – This person is responsible for communicating with shareholders, the press, and other outside entities.
   d. Security – The IS Security team is usually the first responder to any incident. The members of this team are also responsible for providing oversight during containment, eradication, and recovery operations.
   e. IS Support – The support team can:
   f. Assist with containment
   g. Establish alternate methods of information processing when primary systems or network paths are disrupted
   h. Assist with system recovery tasks

3. Physical security – Securing the facility and responding to human intrusions and alerts are the responsibility of this role.

4. Facilities management – Responsibilities include resolving power issues, locating and coordinating the move to alternate facilities, and structural assessments and repairs.

Overall responsibilities of an IRT
Your IRTs have three primary responsibilities:

1. To prevent security incidents
2. To respond to incidents when they occur
3. To take steps after an incident to improve the organization's incident prevention, detection, and response capabilities

The prevention of security incidents is a theme running through the first eight chapters of this book. It's essentially an exercise in managing risk in a reasonable and appropriate manner (see Chapter 3), including:

1. Identification of threat/vulnerability pairs through
    a. vulnerability assessments
    b. penetration testing
    c. vulnerability reports from vendors as well as private and government sources
2. Assessment of the probability that a threat will exploit one or more vulnerabilities
3. Assessment of potential business impact if specific events occur
4. Development of action plans, based on sound risk management principles, to proactively mitigate risk

Once an incident occurs, your IRTs must have the skills necessary to quickly react in a way that minimizes business impact. To accomplish this, each member of the team must understand how to:

1. Analyze incident data
2. Determine the scope and nature of the incident
3. Communicate with other recovery teams

Recommendations as to how each of these activities should be executed are provided later in this chapter.

The IRTs' responsibilities don't end once they complete recovery operations. As we'll examine later in this chapter, post recovery activities are a very important part of incident management. These activities include understanding how to improve prevention and detection controls, how to further reduce business impact, and the development of an action plan to make the necessary adjustments to incident response teams, controls, and documentation.

Incident Management

Develop a communication plan

One of the most important facets of incident management and response is communication. Adequate communication for the purpose of recovery, business impact control, and public relations considerations requires reaching out to various internal and external entities. Figure 9-3 depicts communication points you should consider during preparation, response, recovery, and post-recovery operations. Your incident management communication plan should include names, phone numbers, and when to contact each entity listed. I'm not going to discuss all of these entities; the following is a look at some of the most important.

Figure 9 - 3: Incident Management Communication Points
(Grance, Kent, & Kim, 2004, p. 2-4)

Media – In our description of the members of an IRT, we included a public relations professional. Sending the right message to the media is absolutely essential if you hope to effectively deal with the fears of customers and investors. In addition to the public relations representative, all other members of your IRTs should also be trained on how to respond to inquiries from the press.

Law Enforcement – Develop a relationship with local, state, and federal law enforcement prior to the occurrence of an incident. Use this opportunity to understand how each agency can help and how they prefer you process evidence or a potential information security crime scene. Once an incident occurs, coordinate contact with law enforcement through senior management, human resources, and if appropriate, your legal department.

Incident Reporting Organizations – Although reporting an incident to an organization like the United States Computer Emergency Readiness Team (US-CERT) at http://www.us-cert.gov/ is not necessarily going to improve the quality of your recovery, it will provide information to a central database that law enforcement agencies and businesses can use to identify and mitigate threats or vulnerabilities across the national infrastructure.

Organization's ISPs – Your ISPs, or Internet Service Providers, are an important resource during an attack via the Internet. If you've taken appropriate steps during preparation activities, your ISPs can assist by quickly blocking suspect traffic. In addition, an ongoing relationship with your ISP can result in frequent reviews of the steps they're taking to proactively prevent known attack traffic from reaching your network perimeter.

Owners of Attacking Addresses – In many cases, the systems used to attack your network may be infected machines on an unsuspecting organization's network. Make sure at least one person in each IRT knows how to quickly locate the owner of an IP address by using a service like ARIN (http://www.arin.net/). A quick call to the address owner can accomplish two objectives. First, the owner can block all outgoing traffic associated with the attack. Second, the owning organization can take steps to rid their network of the malware; this will help prevent future attacks.

Before making the call, consider whether you plan to push for legal action against the attacking site. Calling an organization you believe might be an innocent victim could inadvertently result in providing notice to the attacker that you've identified him; this gives him ample time to destroy valuable evidence.

Software Vendors – Before, during, and after an attack, one of the most important communication points is the vendor who supports the target or damaged application or operating system. The vendor can help identify the existence of potential vulnerabilities, recommend critical security patches, translate log entries, provide assistance during an attack, and help with recovery efforts.

Affected External Party – Affected external parties include anyone connected to your network, customers, and vendors. Your organization has a responsibility to practice due diligence to prevent the effects of an incident from migrating to entities connected to your network. Notifying IRTs at connected organizations is a good start. Further, you should let your customers and suppliers know if there will be an interruption in service or product delivery. Finally, if the attack involved the potential compromise of regulated or other sensitive information about employees or customers, it's critical (and in some locations mandatory) to notify all affected parties. Prior to communicating with any external party, be sure to clear the content of the communication through senior management and your legal department.

Incident management preparation might consume significant time and resources. But it provides the foundation necessary to adequately perform the tasks in the remaining incident management steps.

Detect and Analyze

Detection of security incidents requires the implementation of various types of controls—physical, logical, and administrative. Each of these control areas provides layered support to the others. We've examined many of these controls in previous chapters, including:

1. Physical
    a. Motion detectors
    b. Smoke and fire detectors
    c. Security cameras
    d. Sensors and alarms
2. Logical
    a. Intrusion detection systems
    b. Intrusion prevention systems
    c. Logging

3. Administrative

    a. Rotation of duties

    b. Security reviews and audits

    c. Mandatory vacations

    d. Performance evaluations

    e. Background investigations

In this section, we'll walk through some steps that will take your IRTs from detection to a plan for handling an incident.

Once one of your controls provides evidence of a security incident, it's important that you assess what the evidence means. Disconnecting your data center from the network because you get a couple of log entries indicating a malware attack may be okay if you're actually under attack. But what if it was just an explainable and acceptable network anomaly? Explaining loss of service delivery may be difficult if you haven't practiced due diligence before making this kind of decision. Due diligence includes the following steps:

1. Perform an initial assessment to determine the type of incident
2. Develop an action plan to contain and eradicate the threat
3. Document all activities associated with the incident

Once you confirm that an incident is occurring, or has occurred, immediately notify the appropriate IRT. The team's initial response should include a high-level assessment of the following:

1. Initial evidence, including logs and alerts
2. The general state of the system allegedly affected
3. The general state of the network overall

Again, this is a high-level assessment. Digging too deeply at this stage might result in unnecessary delays leading to increased business impact. Using personnel who are familiar with the system, facility, or network being assessed is critical. Individuals who are familiar with day-

Incident Management

to-day characteristics of a potential target should be capable of quickly completing the initial assessment.

Along with the initiation of the initial assessment, the IRT manager should begin documenting all response activities. This documentation tracks details about incident management activities that you can use in post-incident assessments. It also provides a historical record of findings and actions taken, which is often valuable when the exact nature of the attack is hard to identify. The following should be included in your documentation:

1. Current status of the incident – This is normally kept in a running log. The log is a valuable tool for tracking the activities of the IRT, the way in which the attack evolves, and for reporting status to senior management.
2. Summary of the incident
3. Actions taken by all members of the IRTs
4. Contact information for all involved parties
5. List of evidence gathered
6. General observations
7. Pending activities – These should be prioritized based on the criticality of the resources affected; in other words, assess the business impact of not performing each activity on your list. For example, if you need to run payroll the day of the attack, activities surrounding recovery of the payroll system will take precedence over just about anything else.

Again, perform just enough analysis work to get a general understanding of what you're facing. There's a balance between too much analysis and not understanding the incident well enough to effectively contain it.

Contain

Once you understand the nature of the incident, you're ready to minimize its effects. The primary objectives during containment activities are to:

1. Mitigate personal risk to employees and customers
2. Mitigate risk to your business

Secondary objectives include:

1. Collection of evidence
2. Identification of attacker

Note that the most important objective is the protection of people from injury or death. Protection of information processing systems, crime scenes, or the capture and punishment of an attacker are all far less important.

There are various ways to contain a threat. The containment strategy selected depends on:

1. The type of threat
2. The objectives of the attack
3. Potential damage to or theft of resources
4. The need for preservation of evidence
5. The importance of restoring one or more affected systems
6. The opportunity costs associated with a specific strategy – If a single containment activity takes most of your available resources, what additional damage may be caused because you were unable to deal with other effects of the threat?

Strategies you might consider include:

1. Shutting down target systems (i.e., servers, workstations, routers, switches, etc.) – Care should be taken when considering system shut downs. This often destroys evidence. However, powering off systems may be necessary to prevent significant loss of data or to quickly contain a rapidly spreading attack.
2. Disconnect target systems from the network
3. Disable certain services on one or more systems

4. In the case of human intrusions:
   a. Ensure the safety of personnel in your facility.
   b. If you have company security officers on site, take steps to delay the intruder.
   c. Notify local law enforcement.

Containing a threat is essential if you want to have any chance of eradicating it; otherwise, you're trying to hit a moving target.

Forensics

Forensics, or forensic science, is a scientific approach to determining the who, what, when, where, how, and why of a crime. For our purposes, it specifically deals with identifying the perpetrator, causes, and timeline of a security incident. Applying forensic processes during containment may not be practical. As discussed earlier, there are often more important considerations. However, this is a good place in the process to begin thinking about how to balance damage control with collecting the information necessary to prevent or deter future attacks.

It's outside the scope of this book to go into detail on investigative techniques. There are several good books available that address forensics in general and computer forensics specifically. But reviewing the following considerations provides a rough foundation.

Retain your objectivity – Collect data and evidence, conduct interviews, and leave your conclusions until you have enough information to clearly see what actually happened. Jumping to conclusions early in the process usually results in the investigator ignoring anything that seems irrelevant because it doesn't fit with his mental picture of what happened.

Ensure the proper collection and handling of evidence – Much of the evidence you collect may be volatile and difficult to preserve. Be sure to have at least one person on each IRT trained in proper evidence collection, tagging, and storage. Some types of evidence to consider include:

1. Computer screen displays
2. Reports

Just Enough Security

3. Notes
4. System usage patterns
5. Hardware configuration
6. Contents of storage devices, including removable storage devices (i.e., jump drives, tape, etc.)
7. Contents of bags, briefcases, and purses

When collecting evidence from personal areas, be sure to maintain compliance with corporate privacy policies.

From the time evidence is collected to the time it's no longer needed to support criminal or civil action, it must be properly handled. Proper handling begins with collection. As a piece of evidence is initially collected, the following information should be recorded in a chain of custody form:

1. Description
2. Manufacturer
3. Model number
4. IP address
5. MAC address
6. Serial number
7. Any other distinguishing characteristics
8. Name, phone number, title, and signature of the person collecting the information and of each subsequent individual who takes possession of the evidence – This entry should also include the time and date of taking possession as well as the location where the evidence was securely stored.

If a computer is seized as evidence, image the hard disk as soon as possible. Never run computer forensics software on any original storage media. This might diminish the value of the evidence.

Create the image with a "bit level" copy. This ensures that every piece of information is extracted from storage, even data intentionally hidden.

Now that you have the threat under control, it's time to eliminate it from your environment.

Eradicate

It's nearly impossible to define a detailed eradication process general enough to include here. Each attack is unique, requiring a unique approach to eliminating the corresponding threat. Proper preparation prior to an attack, however, will provide you with the tools and external resources necessary to put together an effective eradication plan. Eradication includes:

1. Deleting malware from affected systems
2. Disabling access for compromised user accounts
3. Detention of human intruders
4. Possible arrest or termination of employees responsible for fraudulent or destructive acts
5. Any other action that removes a threat and stops attack activities

The first three steps of incident response—detect, contain, eradicate—are focused on containing the scope of the attack and eliminating the threat. Once these objectives are met, recovery operations begin.

Recover

Recovery operations can actually start once containment is achieved. Recovery of critical systems may be necessary to meet deadlines associated with employees (e.g. payroll) or customers. The important thing to remember is to ensure that the system you plan to recover is no longer exposed to the threat. Your flexibility in simultaneously executing multiple steps during incident response is directly related to the IRT skills developed during training and practice exercises BEFORE an attack occurs.

Depending on the nature of an attack and your ability to quickly identify and contain it, activities intended to recover business systems might include:

1. Reconnecting servers and workstations to the network
2. System restores from tape
3. Complete rebuild of systems
4. Replacement of compromised files or reinstallation of applications
5. Immediate device hardening
    a. Install patches
    b. Change passwords
    c. Reconfigure physical and logical perimeter devices

Again, each attack is different. With each response, your teams should get incrementally better at minimizing the amount of recovery work necessary. This is the purpose of the final step in the incident management process.

Control (Manage)

The activities related to this step take place after all other steps are complete, and all affected systems are restored. The purpose of the Control step is to review the incident and determine how to prevent the same type of successful attack in the future as well as to identify areas for improvement to facilitate faster response and better business impact mitigation. Using documents created during the Detect, Contain, and Eradicate steps, the IRTs seek to answer the following questions:

1. What happened?
2. What was supposed to happen?
3. What are the differences, or gaps, between 1 and 2?
4. What are the reasons for the differences?
5. What controls failed or were missing in the areas of people, process, and technology?
6. What are the lessons learned?

Incident Management

The process of answering these questions and the development of an Action Plan to improve incident detection and response are the elements of an After Action Review, or AAR.

Cause and effect diagram

One of the easiest and most effective methods of tracing the chain of cause and effect is through the use of a Cause and Effect Diagram. There are different approaches to mapping cause and effect. Figure 9-4 depicts the method used in the JES model to diagram an incident. This is a variation on an approach documented by Dean L. Gano (1999). Figure 9-4A is a basic diagram with no controls specified. Figure 9-4B is the same diagram with controls. Let's step through the process.

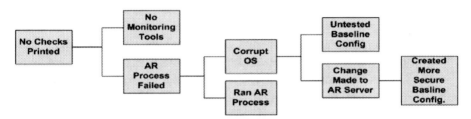

A - Initial Cause and Effect Diagram

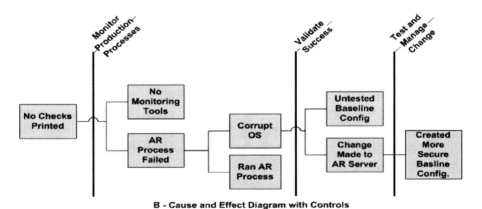

B - Cause and Effect Diagram with Controls

Figure 9 - 4: Cause and Effect Diagram

1. **Begin at the end.** To create a Cause and Effect Diagram, begin at the primary effect on the left and work to the right. The primary effect is the business impact caused by the incident. In our example, it is described as "No Checks Printed."

2. **Ask why.** For each effect identified, ask the question, "Why did this happen?" In Figure 9-4A, the answer is that the "AR Process Failed"; this is the action that created the effect. Notice that there is another box paired with the action, "No Monitoring Tools." This is a condition statement. In many cases, an effect is caused due to an action occurring in the presence of a specific condition. This isn't always the case, but be sure to explore the possibilities carefully. This is considered a condition in this case, because identifying the failure earlier may have provided opportunities to recover and run the checks on time.

3. **Proceed until you reach the point of ignorance or irrelevance.** Continue to ask why until you arrive at a cause/condition pair where any information about what caused them may be unknown or irrelevant when assessing how to prevent the chain of events under analysis. That is where you stop. There is no hard rule for how to identify where to stop. The IRT members will have to make that determination based on the information provided and their knowledge of the business and the technical infrastructure.

4. **Tell the story.** Once you complete the diagram, walk through it from right to left while describing the chain of events leading up to the primary effect. In most cases, you'll want to document this description in an incident report.

5. **Identify failed or missing controls.** As you walk through the diagram, identify where existing controls exist and why they failed. Also identify points in the chain where a new control might serve to stop the progression of cause and effect instances leading up to the primary effect. An important point to remember is that the farther right in the chain you place a control, the more effective you'll be at preventing business impact. Annotate both existing and proposed controls in your diagram. Figure 9-4B is one way you might accomplish this.

Let's walk through our example and see how the incident description might be documented.

> *The security team created a more secure baseline configuration. Without testing the new configuration, a change was made to the AR Server. This*

Incident Management

resulted in a corrupt operating system on the AR Server. The corrupted state of the system went undetected since no validation process was executed to ensure proper operation of the AR Server. When the operators ran the AR process in the corrupted environment, the AR process failed. Since there were no automated tools or manual checkpoints to monitor the health of the AR process, the operators were unaware that the process had stopped. Because no action was taken that would have resulted in a successful recovery of the AR system, no checks were printed.

Notice that there is no assignment of blame anywhere in this description. The fastest way to make your AARs ineffective is to make it a forum for finger-pointing. The AAR process should be professional and objective, seeking only the facts so that improvements can be made.

As we told the story represented by our example Cause and Effect Diagram, it was easy to see the points at which controls were missing. The following is the description again with text in bold that point to missing controls.

The security team created a more secure baseline configuration. **Without testing the new configuration**, *a change was made to the AR Server. This resulted in a corrupt operating system on the AR Server. The corrupted state of the system went undetected since* **no validation process was executed to ensure proper operation of the AR Server.** *When the operators ran the AR process in the corrupted environment, the AR process failed. Since there were* **no automated tools or manual checkpoints to monitor the health of the AR process**, *the operators were unaware that the process had stopped. Because no action was taken that would have resulted in a successful recovery of the AR system, no checks were printed.*

If you compare the missing controls identified in the second iteration of the incident description, you'll see that they are closely related to the conditions identified in the diagram. This is no accident. In most cases, the most effective way to stop an unwanted chain of events is to eliminate one or more unwanted conditions. In our example, no controls existed. We inserted the recommended controls in Figure 9-4B, which we'll use to create an action plan.

Action plan

An action plan is the final product of an incident response. In our example, I would recommend two items for the action plan. First, I would plan for the implementation of a Change Management Process. Change management is a good way to implement change into a production environment while ensuring a low probability that the change will interrupt service delivery. If the engineers in our example follow change management best practices, they will test changes before moving them into production. Further, they will execute a validation process to make sure the AR Server is functioning properly. If the change causes a problem, the engineers will execute a back out process to return the server to its original state. All of these processes should be documented and tested BEFORE the change is made to production.

Second, I would plan for the implementation of either manual or automated processes to track the execution of production jobs. This is another best practice that was missing from our example environment.

This is a very simple representation of how to approach an AAR. Your organization's culture, management hierarchy, and the nature of each incident will affect the way you approach incident reviews. The example used here is more relevant to a Business Continuity event than an attack on your network; but the process of identifying causes and effects is the same no matter where you use it.

CHAPTER SUMMARY

Incident management is a key part of an organization's efforts to maintain accurate, on time service delivery. Building an incident management capability requires careful preparation, complete documentation, and the formation and training of IRTs. Testing incident response scenarios is just as important as testing recovery from potential declared disasters.

The steps in responding to an incident are detection, containment, eradication, and control. The use of cause and effect diagrams to map the course of an incident and the efforts to recover from its effects is an important tool for identifying weak or missing controls. The use of a cause and effect diagram, as part of an overall AAR, leads to the creation and execution of an action plan designed to strengthen an organization's ability to prevent significant adverse business impact due to security incidents.

Works Cited in Chapter 9

Gano, D. L. (1999). Apollo root cause analysis: a new way of thinking. Apollonian Publications.

Grance, T., Kent, K., & Kim, B. (2004). *Computer security incident handling Guide (NIST SP 800-58)*. Retrieved April 1, 2005 from http://csrc.nist.gov/publications/nistpubs/800-61/sp800-61.pdf.

CPSIA information can be obtained at www.ICGtesting.com
Printed in the USA
244621LV00002B/94/A